EXPERIENCING JESUS

Experiencing Jesus

Gerald O'Collins, S.J.

First published in Great Britain 1994
Society for Promoting Christian Knowledge
Holy Trinity Church
Marylebone Road
London NW1 4DU

British Library Cataloguing-in-Publication Data
A catalogue record for this book is available from the British Library

ISBN 0-281-04763-4

Typeset by Datix International Limited, Bungay, Suffolk
Printed in Great Britain by
Biddles Ltd, Guildford and King's Lynn

Contents

Foreword

It has been my privilege to have known Gerry O'Collins for a number of years. As Professor of Theology at the famous Gregorian University in Rome his scholarship is impeccable. But also as a true ecumenist and a gifted teacher he has served his Lord and Church so well in deepening the faith of many. *Experiencing Jesus* allows the reader to share some of those insights as he reflects on various Lenten readings to discover the meaning of Christ's life, death and resurrection in a global context. It is a deeply encouraging book – one which is suffused with hope in Christ, in God, in humanity, in this world and in the world to come. Yet this is no escapist book which avoids the pain and agony of a world in crisis. These issues are confronted whether in Bosnia, or through the eyes of a drug addict, or when facing the death of the very young. Professor O'Collins takes us back, again and again, to the paradigm of the crucifixion of Christ which is portrayed in all its ugliness, yet through it the hope of Easter is born.

This is a book to read and reread – to savour and to meditate upon – and through it to be drawn to experience Jesus more deeply. He ends with the prayer: 'I hope and pray that its readers might experience even more deeply the fullness of life, meaning and love which Jesus holds out to each of us'. I have every confidence that this timely and significant book will enable many to do just that.

† George Cantuar

Introduction

> Remember not the former things . . .
> Behold, I am doing a new thing.
> (Isaiah 43.18–19)

*M*any biblical commentators have detected St Matthew's personal signature in the remark he records from Jesus about every teacher of the law who becomes a learner in the divine kingdom: 'He is like a householder who can produce from his store things new and things old' (Matt. 13.52). It takes, of course, a wise householder to judge when to prefer the new things and when to stick with the old things.

What Matthew wrote here in the first century found its counterpart in a book from the late 1970s by Peter Berger: *The Heretical Imperative*.[1] The American sociologist explored in that work the challenge facing Christians (and practising members of other world religions) in the tension between what they have inherited from the past (the old things) and their experiences in the present where they face the future shock (the new things). In the original sense of the word 'heretical', Christians must discern and decide. They face this imperative and have no other choice but to select what they will produce from their store: the new and/or the old.

In the face of this 'heretical imperative' Berger himself named two false responses: a rigid attempt to recapture the past or sheer capitulation to the present. It is no more a solution to insist rigidly on the past than it is to be swept away by the present. Matthew (and behind him Jesus) encourages us rather to bring out of our store the new *and* the old, in the spirit of both/and rather than either/or.

Among the major treasures we have inherited from the past come the Scriptures, things old which our experience constantly proves to be astonishingly new.

One of the most notable Roman saints, St Gregory the Great, commented that the Bible provides waters in which lambs may walk and elephants may swim. If you like, the Scriptures are waters in which lambs may gambol or play and elephants have a good workout. St Gregory's point is clear. In the Bible there is always something for everybody. Lamblike you can go playing in the water of the Scriptures, or you can have a solid roll around with the Scriptures and imitate a determined elephant off for its daily swim. Maybe not too many of us feel ourselves to be either lambs or elephants; probably we think of ourselves as being somewhere in between. But wherever we place ourselves on the lamb–elephant scale, there is always something old and new for us in the Scriptures—if we are willing to get right into the waters of the biblical texts at first-hand and not merely through the commentaries others may provide us with.

For this coming Lent we might plan on a regular gambol or workout with the scriptural readings assigned for each Sunday or even for each day. We cannot do much better in Lent (or at any time of the liturgical year for that matter) than to follow through on the prescribed readings. My main purpose in this book is simply to open up the run down to the beach, in the spirit of 'come to the waters'. In this introduction

I want to concentrate on two verses from the first reading used in cycle C for the Fifth Sunday of Lent: 'Remember not the former things, nor consider the things of old. Behold, I am doing a new thing' (Isa. 43.18–19; see also 48.6).[2]

Despite these verses from Isaiah, the Scriptures sometimes do invite us to remember former things and consider things of old. Deuteronomy presents Moses as calling on the people to remember former things and confess with one voice: 'A wandering Aramean was my ancestor; he went down to Egypt and lived there as an alien . . . We cried to the Lord, the God of our ancestors; the Lord heard our voice and saw our affliction . . . and brought us out of Egypt with a mighty hand and an outstretched arm . . .' (Deut. 26.5–8). The New Testament itself, notwithstanding its name, can sometimes invite us to consider things of old. In a debate with some Pharisees over marriage and divorce, Jesus asked them: 'What did Moses command you?' After they had given their answer, Jesus went back even further, to the very story of creation itself and the making of man and woman (Mark 10.2–9).

In both cases, Deuteronomy 26 and Mark 10, we might argue that the invitation to remember former things is very much in the service of what people are to do now. The past is recalled because of its present significance. In the case of the creed in Deuteronomy, old things are evoked to make the people ready to give thanks here and now for the Lord's blessings: 'You shall rejoice in all the good which the Lord has given to you' (Deut. 26.11). In his debate with the Pharisees, Jesus calls to mind the original purpose of God in creating men and women, attributes the provisions for divorce introduced by Moses to 'your hardness of heart,' and wants to introduce now a new dispensation for marriage: 'What God has joined together, let no man put asunder.' In both examples, the Deuteronomic creed and the debate with the Pharisees, present attitudes are important. Yet, all in all, the emphasis seems to be put on the lessons to be drawn from the old rather than on anything special the new has to tell us.

At times, however, the Scriptures are more or less even-handed in balancing the old and the new. Matthew, in autographing his gospel with that remark about producing from his store things new and things old, reveals what he intends to do. As an expert in the Mosaic law who has become a disciple of the divine kingdom, he hopes to preserve past truths in the light of Jesus and make something new of them. There is a balancing between the old and the new. As a teacher of the law turned learner of the kingdom, Matthew wants to bring out both. Yet one should notice that Matthew did put new things in first place. There is a preference for the new, even when Matthew names both the old and the new.

Our Scriptures then, can often show a vigorous, almost one-sided preference for new things. Think of the Book of Revelation and its final vision: 'I saw a new heaven and a new earth; for the first heaven and the first earth had passed away ... I heard a loud voice from the throne saying ... "Neither shall there be mourning nor crying nor pain any more, for the former things have passed away." And he who sat upon the throne said: "Behold, I make all things new"' (Rev. 21.1–5). This option for the new in the Book of Revelation illustrates that book's connection with the text I quoted above from Second Isaiah (Isa. 40—66). In fact, many links of language and thought show up between Revelation and Second Isaiah, not least being the theme of the new.

'Remember not the former things, nor consider the things of old. Behold, I am doing a new thing.' This is a very suggestive text about Lent, not only for the Church community at large but also for each of us as individuals. No Lent is or should be like any other Lent. Our spiritual life and experience of God are never meant to be a mere repetition of what has gone before. Through Isaiah's text God is not saying to us: 'Remember the former Lents and consider the Lents of old. Behold, I am doing the same old thing for you.' God is rather saying to us: 'Remember not the former Lents nor consider the Lents of old. Behold, I am doing a new thing this Lent.' God promises to make all things new for everyone: O'Collins, Peters, Taylor, Dempsey, and the lot of us. The temptation against which our Isaiah text should put us on guard is that of drifting into thinking: 'O'Collins yesterday, today and the same forever; as he was in the beginning, is now and ever shall be, faults without end. Amen.' God is rather in the business of making new persons of us. No Lent should be like any other Lent. For the community at large and for us as individuals, the divine guarantee comes through clearly: 'I am doing a new thing. I am making all things new.'

I have indicated a strong stress on the new which we find in a text from Second Isaiah and in a New

Testament book that takes some themes and language from that Old Testament book. But at once I must recognize that in neither case does the new simply crowd out the old. The new heaven and the new earth of Revelation would be unintelligible without the old heaven and the old earth. The language of Second Isaiah about the new exodus makes no sense unless we recall the first exodus. God undertakes to bring the people out of exile in Babylon and lead them through the desert, just as God once made a way for them through the sea and destroyed the pursuing army of Egyptians. The people will appreciate the new thing God is doing only if they remember the former things and consider the things of old. Looking back, far from being forbidden, is in fact strongly implied by our text from Second Isaiah. Remembering with gratitude the old exodus will make the people value even more the new exodus God is bringing about. Openness to the new predominates, but a grateful memory for the past supports it. Far from crowding out the past, the new is fully and properly experienced only by remembering the past.

Hope feeds on memory. Hope for the future and a memory of the past are not opposed. Quite the opposite. Memory supports hope. Remembering their first exodus from Egypt, the people hope that God will lead them once again through the desert on a new and even more wonderful exodus. God was lovingly faithful in the past. God will be lovingly faithful in the future. In delivering the people, God was inventive in the past. God will prove even more lovingly inventive and innovative in the future.

If you have gone along with me so far on this lamblike gambol or elephant-like workout on one passage from Second Isaiah, where does that leave our Lent in this year of grace? God wishes to do a new thing for us—right now in our run up to next Holy Week and Easter. Yet openness to that new thing requires also that we remember our Lents of old. With gratitude and amazement we can also look back at those former things and the old exoduses in our lives. God has led each of us on through the sea. How many times God has brought us through the waters and destroyed the pursuing enemy! A good friend wrote to me recently and signed off, 'as one miracle of grace to another miracle of grace'. We are all miracles of grace. Let us remember in prayer our past and all that the good Lord has done for us in delivering us and bringing us out of the captivity of evil. Openness to God's new thing does not in any way mean turning our back on the past. Rather it means remembering it with immense gratitude, and expecting also to find in it some clues about the new exodus God has in store for us—some clues about the innovative love that God will continue to exercise on our behalf.

A few years ago a book I had committed was shortlisted for a prize. Like any Irish Australian, I got interested in the race and the run past the judges. In the event I was edged out in a photo-finish, but I was not disappointed. The winner was a splendid book, with an excellent title: *The God of Surprises*.[3] That title catches much of what Second Isaiah's text is about. God is doing the divine thing, and it will not be the same old thing but a surprising thing, a new thing coming from our infinitely inventive and surprising God. The title also suggests something about this

Lent. During this holy season, if at any time in the year, God will prove to be a God of surprises who offers us all a Lent of surprises.

Let me draw my elephantine workout or my lamb-like gambol to a close, by recalling how often the Bible proves Matthew to be right, bringing out of its treasure things new and things old, and doing so in that order. Second Isaiah, the Book of Revelation, and so much of the Bible does in fact recall the past with grateful praise for the God who made it what it has been. But our Scriptures edge us consistently towards the future where our surprising God is constantly preparing new things for us. We all live our lives between the old and the new, but the deepest pull must be towards the new.

I have highlighted Second Isaiah. Let me end with its New Testament counterpart, the Book of Revelation and its beautiful phrase for God as 'the One who is, who was and who is to come' (Rev. 1.4,8). The God of our experience, the One who is, proves to be constantly and intimately present to us. The God of our memory, the One who was, led us through our past right down to this point. But it is the future which should predominate, that future which is in the hands of the God of hope, the One who is to come. The phrase from Revelation might have read, 'the One who is, who was and who will be'; it could have kept the verb 'to be' in all three sections, suggesting how God is equally there in the past, present, and future. The small but significant change we find in the text lays just the right stress where it should be placed: on the future. May the God 'who is, who was and who is to come' surprise us all this Lent and bring out of the divine treasure for us not only what is old but also and much more what is wonderfully new.

In this book I want to think about what God offers us in Jesus and in ourselves. Why do we need Jesus? What does he offer us? How do his dying and rising enter into our lives? If what I write helps readers to experience Jesus more vividly and powerfully this Lent, I will be more than satisfied.

I want to register my gratitude to Martin Nolan, Alfred Singer, Peter Steele, and Bishop Rowan Williams for supplying several thoughts which I have developed in this book, and to *America* magazine for publishing an earlier version of chapter 10. My special thanks go to Dominic Maruca, Henry Wansbrough, Brendan Walsh, and his associates for various corrections and improvements to the text. Finally, I am deeply grateful to His Grace the Archbishop of Canterbury, the Most Rev. and Right Hon. George Carey, who as a friend has done me the great kindness of contributing an inspiring foreword.

I dedicate this book to the memory of John Todd, a friend to whom I owe an inexpressibly great debt of gratitude. For years John kept at me to write a book like this. I regret that it is only after his passing to the Lord that I have come up with *Experiencing Jesus*. I hope John approves.

Gerald O'Collins, S.J.
Gregorian University, Rome
23 March 1994

Notes

1. Peter Berger, *The Heretical Imperative*, (Anchor Press/Doubleday, 1979).

2. In 1969, a Roman Catholic lectionary of biblical readings was issued; it has a three-year cycle of readings for Sunday Masses and a two-year cycle for weekday Masses. Occasionally this book refers to the passages chosen by that lectionary, but does not use any version of the Bible throughout. At times the translations are my own.

3. G. W. Hughes, *The God of Surprises*, (Darton, Longman and Todd, 1991).

I

'What's it all about?'

You are dust, and to dust you shall return.
(Genesis 3.19)

Save us, Lord; we are perishing!
(Matthew 8.25)

There is only God's kingdom and, living or dead,
we are all therein.

(Georges Bernanos,
The Diary of a Country Priest)

*S*ome months ago I was watching a well-acted and popular TV soap opera. After taking us through some minor storms in the domestic teacup, the central personality, an attractive wife and mother in her late thirties, looked off in the distance and asked: 'What's it all about?' Her woman friend seemed equally puzzled about the meaning of life and replied: 'You tell me.'

There are still a few years to go before reaching the year 2000. We can feel as if we are going nowhere on our human pilgrimage and are only struggling along to find the point and purpose of it all. We do not seem to belong to this world. We can feel ourselves to be strangers and pilgrims here, homesick for another place where we shall be truly ourselves.

If we pause to ponder the human condition, we may sense two of the deepest truths about ourselves: our precarious grip on existence and our primordial, never satisfied hunger. Let me give a reading of these two truths in turn and see where they lead us.

Many years ago I met a man who appeared to know very little about Roman Catholics and other Christians, apart from one yearly practice which marks the beginning of Lent. He worked in a city office with two Catholics. Every Ash Wednesday they would return after the lunch-hour break with a trace of ash on their foreheads.

Over and above what that practice proclaims about Christian lives and faith, it certainly indicates several troubling aspects of our human situation. When the priest or other minister sprinkles ash on the crown of our head or smears it on our forehead, there is a choice of two brief exhortations: (a) 'remember you are dust and to dust you will return,' or (b) 'turn away from sin and be faithful to the gospel.' We are dust and we are sinners. Exhortation (b) supposes that we need to turn away from selfishness and sin. We will come back to that in a later chapter. It is (a), the first brief warning, which concerns us here.

Ash on our foreheads shows what we are: people of dust and destined to die. Dust not only symbolizes death and dissolution but also stands for what is anonymous and seemingly pointless. Dust is meaningless looking stuff. Unlike rocks we dig up or sea-shells we find on the shore, it has no shape or form. One heap of dust is like another. Grey, transitory stuff, it does not belong anywhere and can be quietly trodden under foot or brushed aside. We are all mortal and heading towards death. Our lives can look pointless and meaningless—like a grey heap of dust about to be blown away.

There is an Arab saying that our life begins as a drop of seed sown in desire and ends as a handful of dust. Thinking about the start of my existence also shows how far it is from certain tenure. Why am I here at all? My mother and father need never have met. Circumstances could so easily have been different and never brought them together. What mysterious human chemistry and divine grace led them to love one another and decide to marry? Then six years into their marriage why did *that* sperm happily join *that* particular ovum to produce me? Other gametes could have united to form another zygote that would have grown in my mother's womb and emerged to take its place on the family and public scene. But that new person would not have been me. I need never have been.

The Jewish Scriptures have a variety of ways for expressing our tenuous toehold on life. One way is through the image of the deadly waters, the forces of evil that seem always poised to submerge us. Through the early chapters of Genesis we follow the story of the spread of evil. God 'saw that the wickedness of human kind was great and that all their thoughts were evil' (Gen. 6.5). What happened then? The waters of the flood swept over human beings; evil came to claim its own.

Over and over again the psalms picture storms, waves and water as conveying the wicked, destructive forces active in the world. They surge in against righteous people, who will be delivered only through the power of God. The psalmist prays: 'Save me, O God! For the waters have come up to my neck. I have come into deep waters, and the flood sweeps over me. Let not the flood sweep over me, or the deep swallow me up' (Ps. 69.1–2,15). It takes God to control the sea and calm the storms: 'You rule the raging of the sea. When its waves rise, you calm them' (Ps. 89.9). Like people caught in a storm at sea we are constantly threatened by evil and annihilation, but God overcomes their power: 'the Lord made the storm be still, and the waves of the sea were hushed' (Ps. 107.29).

We are all Ash Wednesday people, existing between a drop of seed sown in desire and a handful of dust, and menaced all the time by the waters of destruction. We are as transient as a tiny heap of dust blown away by a gale, mere faces who flick by in a passing parade.

On my last visit to Australia I buried a relative who had spent her life in a rich farming area that stretches from extinct volcanoes down to the coast. New-born lambs made patches of white as they skipped about on the brilliantly green fields. Out in the ocean the last whales were playing before heading south to the Antarctic. The roses Gwenda had pruned were growing furiously. But the house stood empty; she was no longer there.

En route back to Rome I flew via London and enjoyed an urban picnic outside Westminster Cathedral. I ate the delicious, little tomatoes John had planted. But he too was gone and I would shortly be celebrating a Eucharist for him inside the Cathedral.

Perhaps the last thing we want to hear is the core certainty about ourselves: death and the ephemeral nature of our existence. The daily death notices in our newspapers summon us to come to terms with our mortality. It is only wishful thinking—more wishful than thinking—to leave death unexamined and somehow imagine that it will never catch up with us.

At this point I can hear my older sister-in-law exclaiming, 'Please be cheerful. Write something positive.' The voice of a dear friend breaks in as well: 'Write about life. After all we only get one go at it.' If I am not going to lose Posey and Dixie, it is time to move on to the second deep truth about ourselves: our hungry hearts.

One of the masterly touches in Franco Zeffirelli's *Jesus of Nazareth* was the way he brought separate episodes together for dramatic effect. He combined, for instance, the feeding of the five thousand with the conversion of Mary Magdalene. A memorable camera-shot picked her out in the crowd as she bit on a hunk of bread before bursting into tears of joy and repentance. With her hands tightly grasping the bread and her moist eyes fixed on Jesus, she knew that her hungry heart had finally found the one who promises: 'Those who come to me shall not hunger. Those who believe in me shall never thirst' (John 6.35). The scene matched perfectly that line from a prize-winning hymn: 'You satisfy the hungry heart.'

We may describe the hungers of our human heart in various ways. Ultimately they seem to assume a triple shape: a primordial desire for life, meaning and love. We hunger and thirst to live. People argue about how and where to find life. But all yearn for life in its full abundance (John 10.10) and pray not to be sucked under by the fearful forces of annihilation. Second, we want things to make sense. Where goals are clear and meaning comes through brightly, we can cope with great, even immense, difficulties. Absurd situations leave us floating aimlessly and without a compass. In the words of Michael Oakshott, 'to be human is to live in a world of meaning; to be without meaning is to be a stranger to the human condition.' Third, we hunger to love and be loved. Love does make our world go round. We yearn to be recognized and encouraged by those who love us. Where love is concerned, our hearts are 'a bottomless gorge', as William Blake put it.

We crave a life that is absolutely full and will never end. We search for a meaning that will light up everything. We hunger for a perfect love that will be utterly satisfying. God is the fulfilment of our primordial yearning. God is the One who will completely and finally satisfy all our hunger and quench our thirst.

The God who saves us from perishing by maintaining us in existence from moment to moment is the God who here and hereafter will fill our hearts. The point and purpose of our existence can only be to praise and thank the God who is our constant, greatest, and most faithful benefactor. Ultimately, that is what it is all about. The only appropriate response is deep and lasting gratitude.

The sense that our whole existence, both now and in the world to come, is sheer gift from God comes through loud and clear in Georges Bernanos' *The Diary of a Country Priest*. The novel repeatedly returns to the same question: what is the basis for our life in the presence of God? How should we interpret our existence?

A young French priest confides to a diary his experiences in a country parish:

My parish is bored stiff, no other word for it. Like so many others! We can see them being eaten up with boredom, and we can't do anything about it. Someday perhaps we shall catch it ourselves— become aware of the cancerous growth within us. You can keep going a long time with that in you.[1]

With simplicity and candour he describes the hopes he entertains and the problems and disappointments he meets in his work for the community and in his contacts with his fellow priests. Physically he suffers a great deal. He burns himself out and eventually will die of stomach cancer.

Along the way the young priest has a dramatic conversation with the local countess. She lost her son when he was eighteen months old; she hates her daughter; and her husband has been unfaithful. Her sufferings have made her bitter. When the countess confesses her bitterness and hatred, the young priest says to her: 'God is not to be bargained with. We must give ourselves up to God unconditionally.' But why should the countess or anyone else follow the priest's advice 'give everything'?

The answer comes powerfully at the end of *The Diary of a Country Priest*. It is because God has first graced us with everything that we owe God everything in return. The whole of our existence is a free gift made by the God who is love. The novel closes when the young priest, already desperately ill from cancer, goes to visit an old school-friend who persuades him to stop overnight. Early next morning his host discovers the priest vomiting great quantities of blood. He describes what follows:

The haemorrhage subsided. While I was waiting for

the doctor, our friend regained consciousness. Yet he did not speak. Great beads of perspiration were rolling over his brow and cheeks. His eyes, which I could scarcely see under his heavy, half-closed lids, told of great pain. I felt his pulse and it was rapidly growing weak. A young neighbour went to fetch our parish priest. The dying man motioned to me to give him his rosary. I pulled it out of a pocket of his trousers; and from that moment he held it pressed to his breast. Then some strength returned to him . . .

The priest was still on his way. I felt bound to express to my unfortunate comrade my deep regret that such delay threatened to deprive him of the final consolations of the Church. He did not seem to hear me. But a few moments later he put his hand over mine, and his eyes entreated me to draw closer to him. He then uttered these words almost in my ear. And I am quite sure that I have recorded them accurately, for his voice, though halting, was strangely distinct. 'What does it matter? All is grace.' I think he died just then.[2]

Through his novel Bernanos articulated brilliantly the faith of St Paul and other Christians: 'By God's favour I am what I am' (1 Cor. 15.10). All is gift, including the very hunger of our hearts for the God who is the infinite plenitude of life, meaning, and love.

Any list of outstanding religious poems in English from the last century includes *The Wreck of the Deutschland* by Gerard Manley Hopkins. Five Franciscan nuns, expelled from Bismarck's Germany, clung together and drowned in a shipwreck off the coast of

Kent during the early hours of 7 December 1875. The report of their death inspired Hopkins' masterpiece which begins: 'Thou mastering me God!' The thirty-five stanzas of the poem develop what these opening words convey about the divine mastery and mercy that are revealed in the terror and loss of our fragile lives.

As with Bernanos' country priest, God masters all of us, bringing us into being without consulting us and calling us home at the hour of death. In the words of Bernanos' hero, we must give ourselves up to God unconditionally, letting God stand at the centre and scrutinize us. The more this divine mastering takes place, the more mysterious and strange becomes the God in whom 'we live and move and have our being' (Acts 17.28). Coming near this God means clearing away the encumbrances that normally mask the incomprehensible divine mystery.

An answer to our TV heroine's question 'What's it all about?', could take the form of 'It's all about God mastering me/us'. Or else we might reply: 'Don't worry about your precarious grip on dusty existence, because it's God who is mastering you, the God whom Hopkins goes on at once to call "giver of breath and bread".' Another answer could be: 'With our elemental hunger for the totality of life, meaning and love, we are searching for the God who has been mastering us all along.'

Yet God can seem as mysterious as the One who spoke to Job out of the tempest (Job 38.1—41.34) and 'the Lord of the living and the dead' to whom the five German nuns went in a storm when the Deutschland sank. It is the presence of Jesus among us that throws light on the divine mystery and in a straightforward way teaches us what it's all about. The following chapters will be given over to Jesus, his programme and the destiny to which he calls us. In him we find our only enduring answer to our deepest questions.

Notes

1. G. Bernanos, *The Diary of a Country Priest*, trans. P. Morris, (Boriswood, 1937), p. 9.

2. *Ibid.*, pp. 316–17; (trans. corrected).

2

Jesus the Meaning

Is not this the carpenter, the son of Mary?
(Mark 6.3)

I count everything as loss because of the surpassing
worth of knowing Christ Jesus my Lord.
(St Paul, Philippians 3.8)

*I*n Rome exuberant baroque architecture won out and
stained-glass windows are at a minimum. Twenty years
of living in this city has renewed my taste for the
Gothic cathedrals of northern Europe. During the
night their huge windows are dark and dull. But with
the dawn, light streams through, the patterns show up
and the colours begin to glitter. In their blues, greens,
reds, browns and yellows, the angels, saints and their
stories come dazzlingly alive.

It takes the light of day to bring out the bright
beauty hidden all along in those patterns and colours.
We cannot see the light, let alone reach out and touch
it. But it sparkles luminously through, brings the
majestic windows to life and fills the Gothic cathedrals
with pools of radiance.

Does this example hold out a way of appreciating
Jesus' impact on us? Without the One who is the light
of the world and the meaning of our existence, everything remains dull and dark. When his light comes
streaming through, colours and patterns show up in
our lives. His brightness brings out the beauty hidden

in ourselves, other people and our world. We do not literally see Jesus; we cannot reach out and touch him directly. But he can light up everything and bring us luminously alive.

The problem may be, however, that like the people of Nazareth (in Mark 6.1–6) we feel we know Jesus only too well. He has become all too familiar for us to hope that he will create glorious, Gothic windows out of our lives right now in this Lent.

In his *Confessions*, St Augustine vividly describes the years before he became a Christian. At one stage he was waiting for a special Manichean teacher who was going to untangle all his difficulties for him. This special teacher, called Faustus, lived out of town. Once Faustus arrived, everything was going to be cleared up. All Augustine's questions would be answered, his problems solved and life would really begin. Of course, when Faustus finally came, none of that happened. Augustine had been suffering what has been called 'the waiting-for-Faustus' syndrome.

The people of Jesus' home town may well have been affected by the same waiting-for-Faustus syndrome. They were expecting someone really special to set them free to live and satisfy their hungry hearts. They were waiting for someone quite extraordinary who could tell them 'what it's all about'. Then Jesus came home and began teaching in their synagogue. Yes, they were impressed by his wisdom and mighty works. But they knew him and his family only too well. He was the carpenter who had done jobs for some of them and had worked on building sites in nearby Sepphoris. They knew his mother Mary and his other relatives. Jesus was too familiar to be able to help them with their puzzles and set them on the road to the fullness of life, of meaning, and of love. He was simply not special enough. And so the people of Nazareth continued to wait for Faustus. Someone else, really exceptional and different, would come one day to answer their deepest questions. Then life could genuinely begin.

Now I wonder whether we too may be suffering from the waiting-for-Faustus syndrome. One day, someone truly special is going to arrive from Bangalore, San Francisco or Kyoto, and that person is going to tell me what it's really all about. One day I will find the book or take the course which is really going to get my spiritual life started for the first time.

If we do suffer from the waiting-for-Faustus syndrome, we just might miss hearing and seeing Jesus right there in the ordinary things and behind the ordinary faces of our daily existence. In the people and the chances that make up our regular routine Jesus has already come. We do not need to hang on, waiting for Faustus. Jesus speaks and acts now through the things and the persons we know all too well. Can we afford to let our lives slip away, waiting for some Faustus? Can we afford to postpone living as we dream about someone or something who will turn up one day, explain it all to us and fix everything up for us? St Paul insists, 'Now is the acceptable time; now is the day of salvation' (2 Cor. 6.2).

For those people two thousand years ago in Nazareth someone special was there and had already been there for a long time. There was no need to wait for anyone else. He was already among them, the most extra-ordinary person the world has ever known. But they missed the opportune moment and the day of salvation, because they missed Jesus.

How do we avoid repeating this mistake? How do we make contact with Jesus in a way that lets him put a pattern on the chaos of experience and light up our lives?

What is called for here is a new beatitude, over and above those recorded for us by Matthew (5.2–12) and Luke (6.20–22). We could shape it this way: Blessed are those who need Jesus, for they will be graced by the vivid light of his presence. Blessed are those who want Jesus, for they will find themselves with him.

Augustine suffered from the waiting-for-Faustus syndrome but his heart was hungry. His elemental need eventually put him in the presence of Jesus. Over three centuries earlier than Augustine, the apostle Paul, out of the hunger of his heart, admitted: 'I count everything as loss because of the surpassing worth of knowing Christ Jesus my Lord.' 'My Lord' should alert us to something important. In the Bible 'knowing' characteristically means much more than mere cognitive knowing or knowing with our heads. The knowing Paul intends here is richer and much more personal than the knowing we claim by saying, 'I know the road to Cambridge'. Very often biblical knowing amounts to what we might speak of as experiencing. This is especially true when it is a question of knowing a person. 'Knowing Christ Jesus my Lord' is practically the equivalent of personally 'experiencing Christ Jesus my Lord'.

This kind of deep, personal experiencing may happen on a one-to-one basis, as expressed here in the Letter to the Philippians, where it is a matter of Jesus

and Paul. Or it may be a question of a group knowing
or experiencing Jesus. Remember what many Samari-
tans in John's gospel say to the woman who is beginning to think of Jesus as the Messiah and encourages
them to meet him. They tell her flatly: 'It is no longer
because of your words that we believe, for we have
heard for ourselves, and we know that this is indeed
the Saviour of the world' (John 4.42). They have seen
and, even more significantly, have heard Jesus and his
words. Their personal experience of him has vindicated
the initial faith which the woman's message has aroused
in them. Their contact with Jesus now underpins the
astonishing truth: he is not simply the Messiah they
have been waiting for; he is the very Saviour of the
world.

This personal knowing or experiencing may then
take a group form. But in John's gospel, as for Paul,
the most striking cases often occur on a one-to-one
basis: some human being face to face with Jesus.
Think of Jesus' question to Philip: 'Have I been with
you so long, and yet you do not know me, Philip?'
(John 14.9). We might add: 'Have I been with you so
long and yet you have not really experienced me,
Gerry, Hilary, Laura, or John?' What is it to experience
Jesus and what is it to experience him over the years?
What does our experiencing Jesus entail?

Probably the most significant point to recall is that
no one finally can do our experiencing for us. There is
no such thing as second-hand experience. Experience
has to be direct and first-hand, or else it simply
doesn't really happen. The vicarious experience af-
forded by figures with whom we identify in a play, a
film or a novel is not as powerful. What ultimately

matters is the 'felt' knowledge of our own experience. The experience of studying at Cambridge, of working in London, marrying an Italian, spending a weekend in prayer or any other experience is something we must do or have for ourselves.

It is the same with our experience of Jesus. We experience him for ourselves or not at all. We pray to him ourselves or not at all. No one else, not even the dearest or closest person in our life, can take our place here. We do our praying to and our experiencing of Jesus personally. No one else can do it for us. When Jesus knocks on our door, it is we who must open it to him. Here we cannot say to another person: 'Please get up and see who is at the door of my heart.'

According to the Book of Acts, there were others around when Jesus met Paul on the Damascus Road. At best they shared only marginally in what happened to Paul. It was Paul himself who was confronted with Jesus and invited to experience him in faith.

In the chapter from the Letter to the Philippians which I have drawn on, Paul twice speaks of 'knowing' or experiencing Jesus. In the verse I quoted above, his knowing Jesus is tied up with his initial experience on the Damascus Road which took place about the year 35—the encounter that made Paul a believer and the great apostle to the gentiles. It was an experience which Paul, writing twenty years later to the Philippians, remembers as surpassingly worthwhile. Then a few verses later the apostle speaks again of 'knowing' Jesus. But this time it is an ongoing experience which he associates with the crucifixion and resurrection: 'My one desire is to know Christ and the power of his resurrection, and to share his sufferings in growing conformity with his death' (Phil. 3.10).

There is Paul, twenty years or more down the track of Christian life from his Damascus Road experience, feeling that he must still know and experience Christ ever so much more. One radical personal experience is never enough in our human and Christian lives. Above all when we are dealing with the experience of other persons, we cannot put our experience into a deep freeze or cold storage. With anyone near to us it is like that. Probably all of us have experienced the beauty and pain in our changing experience of our parents or others very close to us. 'To live is to change and to have changed often is to be perfect.' If the words made famous by John Henry Newman can be pulled out of context and applied anywhere else, it is surely so in the area of interpersonal experience. In our profound experiences of family and friends 'to live is to change and to have changed often is to be perfect'. Those words apply even more to our experience of Jesus. The apostle Paul himself must press on, constantly growing and changing as he continues to experience Jesus and live out of that experience.

Once again St John echoes beautifully what Paul indicates about the ongoing, dynamic and changing nature of our spiritual experience of Jesus. John never uses the noun 'faith' in his gospel but only the verb 'to believe' (ninety-eight times) and such equivalents as 'coming to Jesus' or 'hearing Jesus'. Experiencing Jesus as a believer is never something static or something we can possess. It is something verbal, something that we do and experience—over and over again. Day by day we are called to believe in Jesus, to hear him, to come to him and to experience him. Experiencing Jesus is not, of course, the same sort of thing as experiencing the people we love, live with, or work with even though it is partly through our daily personal contacts with them that we can experience him. Our spouses, children, parents, relatives, friends, and colleagues interact with us in a visible, bodily way that is not true of Jesus. Yet pausing to seek his company, and praying to him each day can let us feel his invisible but real presence in and around us—in a way that is no less intimate and powerful for its being less sensual.

In chapter 3 of Philippians, Paul's second reference to knowing/experiencing Jesus catches superbly the sense of dynamic change and growth entailed by his relationship with Jesus. But the apostle adds something further, which is even more vital. This ongoing experience of Jesus relates above all to his sufferings, death and powerful resurrection.

Paul does not spell out the story of Christ's passion and resurrection from the dead. That story, in various traditions, was being handed on in the early Church and after the time of Paul would enter into our gospels. The Philippian Christians and others in the fifties could have filled out Paul's reference to the suffering, death and resurrection of Jesus by recalling what they knew from the various traditions available to them. Today we can fill out Paul's remarks by giving plenty of time to the final chapters of the gospels. We miss much if we put off confronting ourselves with those chapters until Holy Week and Easter Week. In a very important sense the end is where we should start—with the story of the first Good Friday and Easter Sunday.

Any lasting, interpersonal experience proves transforming. Knowing someone deeply will make us like
him or her. It is not an accident that in happy marriages
men and women come to act, speak, and even look like
each other. His enduring experience of the crucified
and risen Jesus transformed the apostle Paul, making
him also a Good Friday and Easter Sunday person.

In one form or another, life will sooner or later
crucify each one of us. That crucifixion will make us
or break us spiritually. It will certainly be the time
when we cannot escape the question, 'What's it all
about?' We can become fiercely angry at God. Or else
we may vaguely hope for some Faustus to turn up and
explain it all for us. A deep and ongoing contact with
Jesus may not throw meaningful light on everything at
once. But what Paul promises and experience vindi-
cates is that 'knowing' Jesus constantly and intimately
will allow our crucifixion to be transformed into a
strange but powerful resurrection.

The lectionary for this year's fifth Sunday in Lent
sets our passage from Paul's Letter to the Philippians
side by side with John's story of the woman taken in
adultery (John 8.1–11). As we pass from the second
reading to the gospel, the camera—so to speak—swings
around 180 degrees. The epistle is about Paul's encountering Jesus; we look at Jesus through the apostle's
eyes. The gospel, however, is about Jesus encountering
the woman caught in an act of adultery. We look at her
through Jesus' eyes.

The difference between the two passages is much
more, however, than a change of camera shot. In the
epistle, Paul expresses his clear desire to experience
and go 'n experiencing Jesus. Quite consciously and

explicitly, the apostle wants to grow in his experience of Jesus, become even more closely conformed to his suffering and death, and so share in his saving resurrection. In the gospel, however, we have the story of someone who comes to know Christ without wanting to do so. She has a death-and-life experience of Christ but not one that is intended by her. The woman encounters Jesus in a way that brings her suffering and resurrection, but this experience is far from her mind when she gets up that morning. Has she been thinking only of her lover and planning a secret rendezvous with him? If so, the day turns out dramatically different—in terms of her pain and new life.

She is also very different from the Paul of the Letter to the Philippians inasmuch as she seems to be meeting Jesus for the first time. Paul writes of a Jesus whom he has been lovingly experiencing for twenty years or more. The woman, however, has never known or experienced Jesus before. Yet Jesus' impact on her is as startling as the Damascus Road encounter. Her physical life is saved. Her spiritual life is turned around, as she finds someone who deeply cares for her and forgives her. Spiritually she moves through sin, suffering and the threat of death to the promise of new life.

It can be illuminating to compare and contrast Paul with the anonymous woman taken in adultery. The apostle is well known to us. She just surfaces for a fleeting moment in the gospel story; we know so little about her—not even her name. But it is basically the same experience—namely, meeting Jesus—that saves both her and Paul from oblivion and death. We remember this woman and her story, because she meets

Jesus, and through that meeting passes from death to life.

What is true of her and Paul holds good of all of us. It is Jesus who lets us pass from suffering, death and oblivion to a meaningful and everlasting life. It does not ultimately matter how we meet Jesus. We may be knocked to the ground like Paul, or we may be dragged into his presence like the woman taken in adultery. Finally, the only important thing is to know him in the power of his death and resurrection. Then we shall learn 'what it's all about' and pass from death to life.

It is hard to imagine two persons more different than Paul, the utterly dedicated Pharisee who became Jesus' tireless apostle, and the nameless woman seized in an act of adultery. But the lectionary rightly puts them side by side. For all time they are held together by their experience of Jesus, a deep and dramatic experience which both then and now promises to change everything for any of us.

3

Encountering Jesus

I have come to call sinners to repentance.
(Luke 5.32)

He is out of his mind.
(Mark 3.21)

*B*oris Pasternak's moving novel *Doctor Zhivago* covers life in Russia during the first three decades of this century. Early in the novel Lara, still only a schoolgirl, is seduced by a rich lawyer. Desperate and depressed, she visits a church, feeling as if the pavement might open at her feet or the vaulted ceiling collapse on her. It would, she thinks, 'serve her right and put an end to the whole affair'. Her life has become unbearable and she would be glad to die. It is her misery that makes her ready to listen.

In the echoing, half-empty church her cousin was reading at breakneck speed the beatitudes: 'Blessed are the poor in spirit . . . Blessed are they that mourn . . . Blessed are they that hunger and thirst after righteousness.' Lara shivered and stood still. These were words addressed by Christ directly and personally to her. 'He was saying: Happy are the downtrodden. They have something to say for themselves. They have everything before them. That was what he thought. That was Christ's opinion of it.' She no longer felt meaningless and without a future. Even there in a drab and distracting church, Lara knew Christ's gentle promise of mercy. She heard him speaking to her even through the words that someone was rattling off without devotion.[1]

Another novel of this century portrays more violently Christ's ability to touch our lives. At the heart of Evelyn Waugh's *Brideshead Revisited* is the story of Charles Ryder, a non-believer who undergoes a slow, gradual change. His conversion takes years. But when it comes, it happens with great power. At one point Waugh uses the image of an avalanche. The snow and ice build up slowly in the winter. Then the wind drops, the sun comes out, and the thaw sets in. A huge segment of ice and snow opens up, splinters off and thunders down the valley.

We need images like that to describe the power of Jesus to change and convert us. In the gospel for Thursday of the third week of Lent, Jesus himself uses just such a forceful image to express what he is about (Luke 11.14–23). He leads a liberating force which breaks into enemy-occupied territory, captures the headquarters and ransacks it. 'When a strong man fully armed guards his own palace, his goods are safe. But when someone stronger attacks and defeats him, the stronger man takes away all the weapons he relied on and shares out the spoil' (Luke 11.21–22).

Jesus is the stronger one, stronger than any forces of evil, more powerful than any horrible problems which imprison and distress us. But how do I know that this is true? How can I be sure that Jesus really is stronger than even the worst evil? My faith teaches me this. But also I have seen it happen repeatedly in people's lives. Over and over again I have seen his avalanche sweep away all the ice and snow. I have seen him break into enemy-occupied territory and set people free.

We may feel ourselves to be a bit like Charles Ryder in *Brideshead Revisited* or Lara in *Doctor Zhivago*. We may think of ourselves as a hopeless case or a lost cause. But with Our Lord there is no hopeless case, no lost cause. He has come and will come like a great avalanche into so many lives. Certainly evil can be extremely strong. But Jesus is the stronger one. He works as 'the finger of God' (Luke 11.20). And even the finger of God is always stronger than the grip of the greatest evil.

Central protagonists in two outstanding, twentieth-century novels have set this chapter going. Let us turn to a similar case we meet on Saturday after Ash Wednesday (Luke 5.27–32). The Gospel for that day might borrow the title from a book long out of print, *Jesus in Bad Company* by Adolf Holl. This gospel reading contains three familiar elements and one subtle but momentous point that we might easily miss.

There are the familiar themes which we have doubtless grown to cherish. First, Jesus calls Levi, a person who collaborates with a foreign army of occupation, practises extortion and is universally despised because of his profession. The tax-collector responds whole-heartedly: 'He left everything and followed Jesus.' The loving invitation Jesus makes to the outcast draws forth a complete response. Second, Levi puts on a large reception for Jesus. Over and over again Luke's gospel reports parties that Jesus attends or stories that he tells which involve meals. In real life and in the parables of Luke's gospel people are constantly eating, celebrating their joy at being forgiven and their delight in God's friendship which Jesus has brought them. Third, the gospel passage ends with Jesus' words about the radical orientation of life he proposes: 'I have come to call sinners to repentance.' His call is no cheap, bargain-basement offer. It challenges us to let our existence become totally refashioned through the kind of deep change we see in Levi. He drops everything to follow Jesus and then holds a great party to share Jesus with his friends, other tax-collectors whom 'respectable' people loathed as the dregs of society.

These three beautiful elements which shape the story leap out at us: Levi's total response to Jesus' invitation, the feast of joy and the full re-orientation of life which Jesus' call to conversion entails. In all of this we might miss one crucial point in what Jesus says at the very end: 'I have come.' Those simple-looking words lift Jesus quite beyond anything a mere prophet might say. Prophets can assert, 'I was sent,' and in claiming that they implicitly add 'by/from God'. But one who is just a prophet dare not say, 'I have come.' Such an expression conveys divine authority and the promise of a powerful and abiding presence.

We might wish to paraphrase the thrust of the whole story by representing Jesus as saying:

> I have come to call Levi.
> I have come to share the divine presence.
> I have come to invite you all to a profound conversion of life.

Put this way, Jesus' words express a daunting, authoritative challenge. But his encounter with Levi also conveys a comforting promise:

> I have come to call you, but I will make your wholehearted response possible.

I have come to invite you to re-orientate radically
your life, and I will make that change not only
attainable but also the beginning of a feast of joy
that will never end.

Yet who was and is this Jesus who can touch profoundly the lives of Lara, Charles Ryder, Levi and the
rest of us? A provisional account could contain three
themes that stand in certain tension with each other:
Jesus suffered from holy madness; he was deeply rooted
in daily life; he displayed an extraordinary blend of
feminine and masculine qualities. Let me spell out
these three themes in turn.

Early on, Mark's gospel recalls a scene in which
people say about Jesus, 'he is out of his mind,' and his
relatives come 'to take charge of him' (Mark 3.20–21).
Sadly we have probably all met men and women who
were mad and out of their minds. But we may also
have come across those who suffer from holy madness.
We could have been blessed enough to have known
well one or two cases of holy madness. The really mad
are mentally sick. Those who suffer from holy madness
are not mentally sick. Rather they are those who see
things in a remarkable way from God's point of view.
That makes them break social conventions, cut across
ordinary expectations and prove at times profoundly
disturbing to others.

Jesus, to put it mildly, was a chronic case of holy
madness. He saw things from God's point of view, the
point of view of one whose love will never leave us
alone. This made him break social conventions, cut
across the ordinary expectations of his time, and prove
profoundly disturbing to his contemporaries—to the

point that they eventually killed him. It was no wonder that some people, even some of his own relatives, thought Jesus was out of his mind. The surprising thing is that many more people didn't think he was out of his mind.

It is a blessing, sometimes an extraordinary grace, to know chronic cases of holy madness. I remember four or five people whose choices may not provide exact models for other men and women but whose holy madness has permanently affected my own life. One spent his life as a missionary in the west of China, survived wars, imprisonment, floods, and bandits, and died over eighty years of age quietly praying in a chair among the roses at the bottom of a suburban garden. Another turned her back on an academic career to lavish her love on a husband and eight children. Yet there is ultimately no comparison between such cases and Jesus himself, the unique case of holy madness. He was and is the Holy One of God, who being divinely rich became humanly poor for our sake. He laid aside any defences and gave himself to us, because he was beside himself for us. He was and is out of his mind, mad with love for us.

Jesus, while he did seem 'out of his mind,' was also obviously deeply 'in place'. Let me explain what I mean by this second theme. If we took all the images of Jesus' parables and sayings and put them together, we would have a broad picture of daily life in ancient Galilee. There was a hereness and a nowness about the language of Jesus, a vital engagement with the scene right in front of him.

He speaks of stewards running large households, judges administering the law, fishermen sorting out their catch, merchants in search of precious pearls, robbers beating up travellers on lonely roads, farmers harvesting their crops, sick beggars starving outside rich palaces, women mixing yeast into the flour, children playing games in village squares, neighbours arriving home late at night and looking for food. He has noticed women mending torn clothes, rich people throwing big parties, business men unable to repay loans, land-owners building bigger granaries to hold bumper harvests, lilies growing in the fields, and young people playing their parts when friends get married. He knows that sheep can easily stray into the wilderness, that farmers fatten calves for special feasts, and that donkeys and oxen need to be taken every day to water. At times these animals can fall down wells and need to be rescued at once, even on the sabbath day. Jesus notes that cultivating the soil and adding fertilizers might revitalize barren fig trees. Farmers may buy up to five yoke of oxen. Gentile farmers keep pigs and feed them on pods. Jesus is familiar too with popular ways of forecasting the weather, the market-price of sparrows, skins used for different brands of wine, and the safe places for constructing large buildings.

Some of these images come, of course, from the rich storehouse of Jewish Scriptures which he has prayed over for himself and heard read in the synagogue. At the same time, much of Jesus' language suggests an imagination that has scanned a great deal of human living. He is right 'in the place' where he has grown up and worked. By gathering together all his images, we would have a reasonably detailed sketch of what went on in the daily life of Galileans.

Jesus obviously had a very keen eye for his environment. He was intensely alive to the people and the things around him—from kings going to war, farmers piling up manure heaps and growing mulberry trees, right through to tiny sparrows falling dead to the ground. Everything spoke to him of God. His teaching showed how responsive he was to what was happening and how he saw it all as alive with God. He listened to his world and found it sang to him of life with the God whom in his mother tongue (Aramaic) he called *Abba* or 'my father'.

Jesus tells stories of the difficulties farmers meet when sowing their crops, not because he wants to recommend a new method for controlling briars, eradicating thistles, or clearing rocks off the fields. Rather it is because such commonplace scenes as sowing seed on variable terrain reminds him of God's coming close to us and the problems we meet in responding to the powerful presence of the One who loves us infinitely and right where we are. Jesus wants us to look at our Galilee and everywhere find God actively attentive to us. He longs to infect us with his way of being intensely alive to the world and what is happening in it between us and our constantly caring God.

In its own special fashion John's Gospel echoes what we read in Luke by having Jesus declare: 'I came that they may have life and have it abundantly' (John 10.10). Jesus himself was passionately alive to the world around him, a world that brought him the intimate presence of *Abba*. From time to time Jesus did talk of death. But we would distort his message if we were to represent it as 'I came that they may practise death and rehearse it more professionally.' We would be much closer to the truth if we were to sum up his message: as 'I came that they may be constantly alert to God who is always right there where they are and wants to share with them the very fullness of life.'

The third theme that I listed above concerned the unique blend of feminine and masculine characteristics exhibited by Jesus. To identify and distinguish such characteristics means facing controversy almost at every step. But I would not be true to the Jesus whom prayerful reflection on the gospels has shown to me if I did not attempt to do this. Let me share my personal experience here in the hope that it may prove illuminating at least to some readers and not reinforce stereotypes.

The gospel record confronts us with what some see as Jesus' masculine language and characteristics. He looks with anger at those who condemn him for healing a handicapped person. They have made an idol of sabbath observance, and he challenges them by restoring the man's withered hand (Mark 3.1–6). He presents his mission in combative terms: 'You must not think that I have come to bring peace to the earth; I have not come to bring peace but a sword. I have come to set a man against his father, a daughter against her mother, a daughter-in-law against her mother-in-law' (Matt. 10.34–35). The same sense of masculine divisiveness turns up in another saying: 'He who is not with me is against me, and he who does not gather with me scatters' (Matt. 12.30). Jesus is bent on radically changing the environment he has encountered: 'I have come to cast fire on the earth' (Luke 12.49). In Jerusalem he resolutely drives out of the temple those who defile the sacred precincts by using them to do business and making money (Mark 12: 15–17). He fights and overcomes the forces of evil (Matt. 12.22–29). John's gospel, while remaining silent about Jesus' exorcisms or delivering people from the grip of demonic powers, expresses this masculine struggle through the theme of light overpowering darkness (John 1.4–13; 9.1–41).

Alongside such masculine characteristics, we can easily uncover what some people identify as feminine ones. Jesus receives into his presence and nurtures little children (Mark 10.13–16). He is remembered as being utterly at ease with himself and constantly cultivating the inner life of prayer (for instance, Mark 1.12–13,35; 6.46). His sayings include some that seem downright feminine or at least do not find support in the male logic of conflict and competition for prizes: for example, 'whoever wants to save his life will lose it, but whoever loses his life for my sake and for the gospel's will save it' (Mark 8.35). 'Seek and you will find; knock and the door will be opened to you' (Matt. 7.7) sounds like masculine advice and the way to win. But letting go and losing because one hopes to be saved converges with the non-violent, feminine strength-in-surrender with which Luke portrays the death of Jesus: 'Father, forgive them . . . Father, in your hands I commend my spirit' (Luke 23.34, 46).

A striking testimony to the untroubled feminine delicacy of Jesus' language emerges when we recall the image of female prostitution used at times by the Old Testament prophets to focus the disobedience of God's people. The vivid, ugly allegories of sexual infidelity developed by Ezekiel (Ezek. 16.1–63; 23.1–49) more than hint at the male insecurity or dominance of that prophet. Jesus never needs to indulge in such language. On the contrary, he does not flinch from applying to himself a very homely, female image (Luke 13.34). He is present like a mother hen who shelters her chickens when they run back under her wings. Like lady wisdom (Prov 9.1–18) he invites his audience: 'Come to me, all you who labour and are heavily burdened, and I will give you rest' (Matt. 11.28). He will feed them with a wisdom which eliminates false and sinful burdens and gives life in abundance.

Lastly, we can list among Jesus' feminine traits the deep, compassionate tenderness which consistently drew him close to those who suffer. Luke recalls him as having wept over Jerusalem and its coming sufferings (Luke 19.41), John as having wept at the death of his friend Lazarus (John 11.35). Jesus was so 'moved with pity' at the sight of a leper that he touched him and healed him (Mark 1.40–42). Mark's gospel tells also of how Jesus' 'heart went out' to a large crowd of people because 'they were like sheep without a shepherd'. He cared for them, body and soul, first teaching them 'many things' and then feeding them miraculously (Mark 6.34–44). Luke describes how Jesus was 'moved to pity' when he met a widow burying her only son (Luke 7.13). That same gospel brings us Jesus' parable of the merciful father who acted like a mother when his 'heart went out to' the returning prodigal (Luke 15.20). There is no need to ask about the prodigal's mother; his father acts just like a mother.

Having looked at Jesus in the light of one version of masculine and feminine characteristics, I should also recognize that human beings can and do often behave quite differently. Women may exhibit authentically feminine and motherly forms of combative, competitive, and divisive behaviour. Men may exhibit authentically masculine and fatherly forms of nurturing, non-violent and compassionate behaviour.

This Chapter has cited people from real life and fiction whose lives were changed by Jesus. It looked at several striking features in his portrait from the gospels. All of this leaves us with the question: What are some of the details in his programme for us? What if we let Jesus come into our lives?

Notes

1. B. Pasternak, *Doctor Zhivago*, trans. M. Hayward and M. Harari, (Pantheon Books, New York, 1960), pp. 44–45; (trans. corrected).

4

'You leave Jesus out of this!'

Behold, a glutton and a drunkard!
(Matthew 11.19)

You are the Holy One of God.
(John 6.69)

A friend of mine has ministered for years in a part of
the world bitterly torn apart by murderous strife. One
day he was begging a parishioner not to be consumed
by hatred. He bluntly asked the man: 'What would
Jesus think of your attitude?' Quick as a flash came the
answer: 'You leave Jesus out of this!'

We can deliberately 'leave Jesus out of this'. But
then we may be more likely to realize what we are
doing. We know that we are shutting our ears to his
words, turning away from his presence, closing our
eyes to his glance, and refusing to let him touch us and
heal us. A subtler problem may be created by the ways
we let Jesus come into our lives.

We have different pictures of Jesus and different
names for him. Many people wear a tiny crucifix or
keep at home a picture of the crucified One. Others
prefer the image of him as baby in Bethlehem or
preacher of the Sermon on the Mount. Or else they
follow Fra Angelico, Rembrandt and other great artists
by representing him as risen from the dead, meeting
Mary Magdalene and breaking bread with his two
disciples at Emmaus. There is a wide variety in the
names we like to give him. Our favourite name could

be 'Suffering Servant', 'the Son of man', 'the Good Shepherd', 'the Sacred Heart', 'Wisdom of God', 'our Mother', 'Christ', 'Lord', or 'Son of God'. Or else we may remember what the name he received at birth means ('God saves/has saved') and go along happily calling him simply 'Jesus'.

Various views of Jesus support these different images and names. None of us takes over Jesus, or rather is taken over by him, in exactly the same way. Some see Jesus as their best friend, the One who will 'support them all the day long until the evening comes'. Others appreciate him as divine healer, the Son of God working among us and bringing forgiveness to the sinful and sorrowful. Others again view him as the One who stood prophetically for truth and love, only to be crushed at the end by the forces of greed and hatred.

Different passages of the gospels promote and vouch for these and other views of Jesus. The gospels resemble a book of photographs, hundreds of studies of the same subject caught in numerous, distinct 'poses'. We see Jesus acting as baby, child, friend, healer, prophet, master, mother, victim, and risen Lord. Shepherds greet his birth, teachers in Jerusalem wonder at his wisdom, lepers experience his healing touch, crowds marvel at the power of his words, sinners rejoice at his presence and pardon. He takes children in his arms, uses a whip to clear the temple, weeps at the death of a friend, stretches out his arms on the cross, and then comes at dawn to surprise his disconsolate disciples.

The gospels offer various glimpses of Jesus that differ even to the point of appearing incompatible. He speaks the language of a revolutionary prophet who will bring divisions into families by setting children against their parents and parents against their children. Yet angels announce divine peace at his birth, and on the eve of his death he promises his disciples: 'Peace I leave with you; my peace I give you' (John 14.27). He eats with the riff-raff and the reprobate of society, and proclaims God's mercy to them: 'I have come to call sinners' (Mark 2.17). But he also condemns the self-righteous and lashes wrongdoers: 'You hypocrites, you white-washed sepulchres' (Matt. 23.27). Like Matthew, Luke pictures Jesus as warning against the religious difficulties created by wealth (Luke 18.25 = Matt. 10.25). Yet the same gospel repeatedly pictures Jesus as dining out with the wealthy.

There is a strange diversity, even tantalizing elusiveness, about what Jesus says and does in the gospels. We can never really pin him down, stick some label on him and say, 'That's what he is.'

Remembering an accusation levelled against Jesus' followers, 'these people have turned the world upside down' (Acts 17.6), we may think of Jesus as a disturber of the peace or even as the revolutionary of all time. But then we need to remember that he never declares, 'The streets are ours.' If he says, 'I have not come to bring peace but a sword' (Matt. 10.34), it is not a sword in his own hand. A despised 'man of sorrows from whom others hide their faces' (Isa. 53.3), this victim is also a party-goer who eats and drinks with sinners so often that sour critics scorn him as 'a glutton and a drunkard' (Matt. 11.19). The man of sorrows is also a man of joy, who urges his audience to rejoice over God's intimacy and mercy and whose risen presence fills his disciples with joy (John 20.20). The Jesus who goes about 'doing good' (Acts 10.38) has encouraged some contemporary Christians to name him 'the man for others'. Yet he is more than an archetypal do-gooder. He works *for* others, but he also calls others *to* himself and to be *with* him (Mark 2.13–14).

The people of Israel were forbidden to make images either of God or of human beings, formed in the divine image and likeness. The New Testament knows no such prohibition. We can and do make our images of Jesus, inevitably shaping our pictures according to our needs and fashioning them in the light of our convictions. We should all have our cherished images of Jesus, even if we are liable to let our images misrepresent him.

Some years ago a deacon, who belongs to an Eastern rather than to the Western, Latin rite, was taking a course with me on Christ's being and doing. Instead of writing a paper, he chose to paint an icon and present it to the class. When he unveiled the icon, stood alongside it and began to speak, my eyes flicked from him to the face of Christ he had depicted. 'That's also Joe's face shining forth from the icon,' I thought. The face of the artist blended intricately with that of Christ.

Far from being surprised at this story, we should expect our efforts to parallel what deacon Joseph did. Searching for Jesus means searching for ourselves. Truly finding him, or rather being found by him, means finding our true selves. Strangers to him, we remain strangers to ourselves. St Augustine catches beautifully the double nature of our search when he prays, 'Lord, that I may know myself! That I might know you!'

Matthew's version of a scene at Caesarea Philippi illustrates how we ourselves are necessarily involved when we respond to and recognize Jesus. Simon identifies Jesus: 'You are the Christ, the Son of the living God.' This act of recognition prompts Jesus into declaring, 'Simon, son of Jonah, I say to you: you are Peter, the Rock' (Matt. 16.13–18). In this exchange Simon cannot identify Jesus without himself being identified and receiving his new name and function as the Rock. Like Peter, if we respond truly and sincerely to the question, 'Who do you say that I am?' we will become aware of Jesus giving us our genuine identity and true name.

Perhaps our exchange will share that mysterious privacy symbolized by the gift of 'a white stone, with a new name written on the stone which no one knows' except those who receive it (Rev. 2.17). For years I have treasured and kept on my prayer-stool a white stone I came across on an Adriatic beach near the shrine of Loreto. It embodies my hope one day to see Jesus gloriously alive and victorious and to receive through that vision my final identity and name. One's interchange with Jesus may be observed only by a few people, as was the case with deacon Joseph introducing my class of thirty or so students to his icon. We saw how in painting the face of Christ, Joe has also painted, expressed, and found himself. Or else the reciprocal identifying may involve even millions of believers, as happened with Simon Peter. His new name has gone around the world. No matter who or how many witness the interchange, identifying Jesus entails identifying who we are and what we hope to be. Coming home to Jesus is coming home to ourselves.

For the first five centuries of her existence the Christian Church wrestled with the question Simon Peter faced: 'Who do you say that I am?' The Church at large found her collective identity by responding: 'You are truly divine and fully human.' Both parts of the answer have proved and prove essential when identifying Jesus.

To acknowledge him as divine is to receive in him God's self-gift, the reality of God in person or, in Matthew's terms, 'Emmanuel, God with us' (Matt. 1.23; 28.20). He is not just God's fully empowered representative who tells us about God and embodies the divine purposes for our salvation. He is the divine Gift-in-person. He comes to share with us eternal life because that life already belongs to him by natural right. He can tell us about God because he knows about God from the inside.

By recognizing Jesus as truly divine, Christians are justified in adoring him—that is to say, giving him the worship appropriate only to God. They are also justified in drawing a consoling conclusion from their belief. God so valued us and our world that the Son of God entered it in person. By taking on a human existence, the second person of the Trinity showed what we mean to God. The alternative, a Jesus who is not personally divine, means that God was really unwilling to become human and did not after all set such a high value on us.

Years ago I attended a rally featuring the American evangelist and itinerant preacher, Billy Graham. His voice still rings in my ears as he reached his climax and quoted John's gospel: 'God so loved the world that he gave his only Son' (John 3.16). Graham's punch-line would have sounded terribly flat if the gospel had supplied him with a different text: 'God so loved the world that he sent yet another prophet.' We would not have been much more impressed if John had written: 'God so loved the world that he sent us a fully empowered representative.' Nothing can substitute for self-gift and presence-in-person. It is precisely such a divine self-gift and presence-in-person that John wrote about, Billy Graham preached and Christians accept in Jesus.

Alongside his true divinity, Jesus' full humanity also enters essentially into what faith identifies in him. Christians believe him to be genuinely human and not superhuman. No cool, impassive figure, he weeps in painful frustration over the city which has refused to hear his message (Luke 19.41). Exhausted by his preaching ministry, he stays sound asleep on a storm-tossed fishing boat (Mark 4.38). He looks with anger at those whose hard hearts would not tolerate healing a handicapped person on the sabbath (Mark 3.5). Jesus is not ashamed to admit limits in his human knowledge (Mark 5.30–32; 13.32). Luke does not hesitate to acknowledge that Jesus went through the normal processes of human growth (Luke 2.40,52).

It is obviously vital for us that Jesus is truly and fully human. By taking flesh (John 1.14), the Son of God experiences at first hand what it is to be human— with all its limits, including the final, great limit of death. As one of us he can encounter and love us. At the same time, he can also represent us before God, because he belongs to us by sharing completely our condition in life and death. An extraterrestrial alien, who does not share with us from the inside, could not appropriately represent us human beings. It is essential for the Letter to the Hebrews that as our great high priest, Jesus has taken part in our struggles, sufferings, and temptations (Heb. 4.15; 5.7–10).

What may make Jesus' humanity problematical for us is hinted at by John's version of the confession made by Simon Peter: 'You are the Holy One of God' (John 6.69). The problem becomes blatant when the Letter to the Hebrews describes Jesus as 'being tempted in every respect as we are' but then adds that this happened without his falling into sin (Heb. 4.15). Jesus' perfect holiness can seem to tamper with his full and true humanity.

I can still recall the look of scepticism that crossed many faces when a year or so after being ordained a priest, I preached my first sermon on All Saints' Day and began by saying: 'I want to consider with you how sanctity involves our becoming full human beings.' I quickly sensed the difficulty many people feel in their bones, even if they never express it clearly in their minds, that holiness has the opposite effect: it dehumanizes.

Pope John XXIII had died shortly before my maiden sermon on All Saints' Day. His rich, affectionate humanity made its appeal around the globe. But it surprised very many people that such humanity could be found in the most prominent Christian figure of the world. After his death an eminent journalist expressed the wish that John would never be canonized a saint, since this would make him appear less human than in fact he was. That statement implied the widely held belief that holiness does not genuinely perfect our humanity. At bottom we can have the sneaking feeling that sainthood and holiness probably make a man or a woman less of a human being.

Yet the truth is rather that holiness enhances our humanity as nothing else does. Jesus' own perfect holiness made him genuinely and fully human. He wants to transform us into his own likeness, making us holy and so helping us become richly and satisfyingly human. His divine power can turn his wish into a reality.

How does Jesus go about making us holy—that is to say, truly whole and fully human? He does it in two ways, by breaking us down and building us up.

First, he refuses to let us rest until we have become what we should be. We commonly and sometimes acutely experience suffering and discontent. We may try to smother those experiences and anaesthetize ourselves against them. Yet our unrest, our sense of apparent futility and our feelings of staleness persist; this can be Jesus' way of refusing to let sleeping dogs lie. He insists that we be no less than what we can become. He refuses to allow us stay as we are, only half-people who have not yet grown into our full human and spiritual maturity. What he does everywhere today we see him doing in the gospel pages. He shakes and shocks people into breaking with false habits and turning away from what cannot enhance their lives.

Second, Jesus longs to build us up into richer human beings, persons who pray, forgive and act with compassion: in short, people who reach out with love towards God and neighbour. The next chapter will explore some central features of this programme. Here let me merely insist that we need not fear Jesus' call to holiness. Essentially it is a call to love and to a life that enriches and never dehumanizes.

Holiness, far from taking anything away from us, will only add to our lives. Here my choice example is that of St Thomas More. Shortly before his execution his daughter Margaret pushed past the guards to give him a last embrace. From the Tower of London he wrote one of the most touching letters a father ever wrote to his daughter, telling her among other things, 'I never loved you more than when you kissed me last.'

None of us wants to 'leave Jesus out of this'. But every now and then we need to scrutinize the ways we let him into our lives. If we make too much of his sufferings, let us remember the joyful friend who celebrated with repentant sinners. If we habitually think only of his mild gentleness, let us remember his power to challenge and disturb.

Years ago a great scholar pictured God as 'the ever greater God'. No one can ever pin God down; God always remains infinitely greater than all our thinking and imagining. Christ himself, the God-man, is the ever greater Jesus, who goes beyond all that we can think and imagine. May this ever greater Jesus, bringer of true peace and disturber of false peace, stay with us forever, blessing us all and constantly challenging us all. May we never 'leave him out of this'.

5

Loving, praying, and forgiving

Go and do likewise.
(Luke 10.37)

Ask and you will receive.
(Luke 11.9)

*O*n an agreeable evening in Sydney back in the 1960s, I was walking down a suburban street with one of my sisters and a female cousin of ours. A man was sitting on the footpath, his feet dangling into the gutter and his body gently swaying backwards and forwards. The smell of spirits caught us as we walked by. Half an hour later the three of us came back along the same street. An ambulance crew was loading the man on board. He was drunk all right. But he had been sitting down because a car had hit him, broken his leg and failed to stop.

'We have just repeated the parable of the Good Samaritan,' my sister commented. 'Only this time, instead of a priest and a Levite passing by on the *other* side, it's been a case of a priest, a social worker and a nurse passing by on the *same* side' (see Luke 10.29–37).

Many Christians and others have found it attractive to take approval as the primary aspect of love. To love people is, in a most radical way, to approve of, joyfully wonder at, and assent to their existence. The lover rejoices over the object of his or her love and in effect says: 'It is beautiful that you exist, that you are there in the world. I want you to exist. I approve of you utterly.' Unquestionably one can appeal to the Bible in support of this approach to love. After all, when human beings were created in the divine image and likeness, God saw that 'all' was not only good but even 'very good' (Gen. 1.31). With the crowning phase of creation men and women were there, persons to whom God could say, 'I want you to exist. I approve of you unconditionally.'

Nevertheless, the New Testament relentlessly preaches love as active rather than simply approving. To love is to be engaged selflessly for the good of others and work for their welfare and real happiness. When Jesus tells the story of the Good Samaritan, he twice insists on love being active in the service of God and any neighbours we come across in need of us on the road of life: '*Do* this, and you will live . . . Go and *do* likewise' (Luke 10.28,37).

St Paul and St John weaken nothing of this insistence on the call to reach out actively in love. In the original Greek in which he wrote, Paul's famous hymn to love uses fifteen verbs to put forward the active ways through which love expresses itself (1 Cor. 13.4–7). Verbs point to action, the ceaseless activity of one whose patience and kindness know no limits. The First Letter of John likewise endorses the call to act lovingly: 'love must not be a matter of words or talk. It must be genuine, and show itself in *action*' (1 John 3.18).

It is only here and there that the gospels of Matthew, Mark and Luke talk explicitly of love. When questioned about the greatest commandment of the law, Jesus responds by combining two quotations (Deut.

6.4–5; Lev 19.18). The first text stresses the obligation to love God with all our resources: 'You shall love the Lord your God with all your heart, and with all your soul, and with all your mind, and with all your strength.' Even though he is asked only about the first commandment, Jesus at once adds the second: 'You shall love your neighbour as yourself' (Mark 12.28–34). The theme of love connects both commandments: in an original way Jesus juxtaposes the two commandments, one vertical (towards God) and one horizontal (towards our brothers and sisters).

Jesus' own activity exemplifies stunningly a vertical relationship towards the God whom he calls *Abba* and a horizontal relationship towards human beings. The gospels of Matthew, Mark, and Luke depict a life totally energized by love.

First, the ministry of Jesus expresses itself in a dialogue of love and obedience towards *Abba*. In a reckless way Jesus gives himself totally to the service of the present and future rule of God, the final offer of salvation for sinful and suffering men and women. He identifies himself with the divine concern to forgive and save human beings. This loving obedience reaches its climax in the garden of Gethsemane where Jesus prays: *Abba*, Father, all things are possible to you; remove this cup from me; yet not what I will, but what you will' (Mark 14.36).

From the Father's side there came unqualified approval. In an account of Jesus' baptism Mark reports a voice from heaven: 'You are my beloved Son; with you I am well pleased' (Mark 1.11). At the transfiguration of Jesus a voice 'from the cloud' told the three disciples: 'This is my beloved Son; listen to him' (Mark 9.7).

But this reciprocal relationship of love seemed to reach its end on the cross. When Jesus cried out, 'My God, my God, why have you abandoned me?' (Mark 15.34), there was no reply from heaven.

Second, in addition to the vertical dialogue of obedience which made Jesus utterly subject to his Father's will, on the horizontal level this love also drove him to be completely available for the service of those who needed mercy and healing (Mark 10.45; Luke 22.27). When the gospels of Matthew, Mark and Luke report Jesus' ministry, they rarely talk in explicit terms of love (Mark 10.21). Nevertheless, they summon up an activity inspired by love. Jesus rejected no one but gave himself away in love for all. This self-giving proved to be not only dangerous but also deadly. It meant pain when others refused to respond (Luke 13.34; 19.41), loss of freedom (Mark 14.46) and finally the radical diminishment of death.

Jesus not only issued a call to love vertically and horizontally, but he also lived such a love to the full. His crucifixion, however, looked like the final victory for hatred. A later Chapter will face this question. Here I want rather to underline the centrality of self-giving love as the heart of Jesus' programme.

The weekday gospel readings for the first week of Lent begin with a very serious warning about the end of all things. We will be judged on our performance in that practical love which feeds the hungry, gives a home to refugees, clothes the naked, helps the sick and visits prisoners (Matt. 25.31–46). Four of the subsequent readings in that first week come from what has normally been understood to be Jesus' plan-for-life *par excellence*, the Sermon on the Mount in Matthew 5— 7.

It summons us to imitate God by excluding no one and being kind-hearted to all, right through to the limit case of loving our enemies and praying for our persecutors (Matt. 5.43–48). Jesus asks us to go out of our way and do good to our enemies and not simply tolerate them or avoid taking revenge on them. He does not deny that they may well have done us much harm, yet he calls on us to act lovingly towards them.

Nothing can replace the exercise of such love. The Sermon on the Mount draws to a close by warning those tempted to take refuge in the official faith or in their own spiritual gifts. Those who profess the traditional orthodoxy of the Church through believing in Jesus are cautioned: 'Not everyone who says to me "Lord, Lord" will enter the kingdom of heaven.' Even those who have received special charisms to prophesy, exorcise and work miracles are warned:

> When the day comes, many will say to me, 'Lord, Lord, did we not prophesy in your name, drive out demons in your name, and in your name perform many miracles?' Then I will tell them plainly, 'I never knew you. Out of my sight; your deeds are evil' (Matt. 7.22–23).

To enter the divine kingdom it is not enough to profess orthodox faith or even exercise extraordinary spiritual gifts. One must 'do the will of my heavenly Father'—something that is intimately linked, as the Sermon on the Mount makes plain, with hearing the words of Jesus and *acting* on them. One must pass from being a hearer of the word to being a doer of the word. The most demanding words from Jesus concern his invitation to practice boundless love towards all.

The exacting and costly nature of this call justifies G. K. Chesterton's famous quip: 'Christianity hasn't been tried and found wanting. It has been found hard and not tried.' How can we cope with Jesus' challenge to take a plunge on his programme and give everything for love? Where can we find the power to live the kind of self-forgetful love Jesus expects from us?

A feature of Luke's writing may offer us the answer we need. The feature I have in mind is his habit of introducing doublets, two sections that match each other and clarify each other. Over and over again in Luke's writing we come across such doublets: passage A which says something important to us, and then passage B which adds something equally important to fill out what we have already heard in passage A.

Luke alerts us to an example of such doublets when he introduces two distinct stories with the very same question, 'what shall I do to inherit eternal life?' In the first story a lawyer hears the parable of the good Samaritan and is told to '*go* and do likewise' (Luke 10.37). In the second a ruler is invited to give all he has to the poor and then '*come*, follow me' (Luke 18.22). The identical question produces two seemingly different answers. The first man is sent away to care for wounded travellers and any other human beings in distress. The second is called to get rid of his possessions and spend his time in the company of Jesus. But on closer scrutiny the two invitations can be seen to complement and support each other rather than proving mutually exclusive. Those who live in loving and prayerful familiarity with Jesus will have the strength to go and imitate the selfless compassion of the good Samaritan. Those who generously and actively serve their neighbours will do so because prayer has shown them the face of Jesus in the sick, the refugees, the old and the dying. They can *do* 'something beautiful for Jesus' because they have looked on his face in prayer.

At the end of the day it is only persevering prayer that makes it possible to live up to Jesus' programme of love.

Not everyone has noticed St Luke's habit of introducing doublets. But very many of his readers recognize how he emphasizes the theme of prayer. His gospel opens and closes in the Jerusalem temple, which he reverences as the central place of worship in the heart of God's holy city. In his first two chapters, Luke not only frequently refers to prayer but he also gathers together the *Benedictus*, the *Magnificat* and the *Nunc Dimittis*. No other section in the entire New Testament contains anything like the rich chorus of prayer with which Luke introduces his account of Christ. The angels join Zechariah, Mary, Simeon, Anna, and the shepherds in praising and thanking God who offers salvation through Jesus and his message. In effect Luke says to his readers: 'If you approach my book about Jesus with praise on your lips and prayer in your hearts, you will understand who he is and the agenda he sets before us.' Luke is not interested in bringing in songs of praise from angels or anyone else just to make the birth of Jesus sound more extraordinary and impressive. His intention is clear. He wants us from the outset to join in the cries of 'Blessed be the Lord, the God of Israel', 'My soul proclaims the greatness of the Lord', and 'Glory to God in the highest'.

Along with prayers of praise and thanksgiving, Luke encourages his readers to take Jesus seriously when he says to us: 'Ask, and you will receive. Seek, and you will find. Knock, and the door will be opened to you' (Luke 11.9). Jesus guarantees that persevering prayer will be answered. It is impossible to imagine that God would refuse the request of anyone who steadfastly begged for the grace to live out Jesus' mandate of love. Do we fail to receive this power because we do not tirelessly ask for it? Do we miss out on finding love because we do not seek it? Does the door to selfless love stay closed to us because we are not persistent in knocking? If we really want the grace of love, we will keep rapping on God's door like the man who comes looking for three loaves in the middle of the night and eventually irritates his neighbour into getting up and giving him what he wants (Luke 11.5–8).

I hope my Benedictine friends won't be too upset if I suggest tampering with their motto '*ora et labora* (pray and work)' and make it read '*ora et ama* (pray and love)'. Several years ago on a country train in Italy I heard a little Italian girl cheer up a whole carriage. The six-year-old redhead—yes, Italians can also have red hair—kept singing over and over again in her piping voice the refrain of a current hit, '*dammi amore* (give me love)'. It is hard to think of a better petition to make to God. Dear reader, why not take a little time out at this point and test your Italian by saying over and over again to God '*dammi amore*'? That can't do any harm. If we keep up the refrain like that Italian child on the train to Castel Gandolfo, God must make it easier for us to answer Jesus' daunting call to love.

Nothing has verified for me more poignantly just

how demanding Jesus' programme of love really is than some remarks I heard from young people in former Yugoslavia. 'Our priests tell us to love and forgive. But what happens when we forgive? We are pushed out of more villages. Does forgiveness mean that we all have to go off and live in Germany or somewhere else?' Our world needs forgiveness between whole nations and large groups who continue to savage and kill each other with irrational ferocity. But we cannot expect forgiveness on a grand scale between peoples and races, if we fail to practice it on a small scale in our own lives.

G. K. Chesterton once remarked, 'I find it easy to love Eskimos, because I have never seen an Eskimo. But I find it hard to love my neighbour who plays the piano over my head too late at night.' We all have something to forgive, perhaps much to forgive, and it won't be as trifling as someone on the floor above us who plays the piano into the night. It may be our parents who need our forgiveness. It could be someone who has persistently treated us as if we were a thing and not a person. It may be a case of friends and close relatives who have betrayed us. Forgiveness is difficult and costly. In one of his novels Jean-Paul Sartre caricatures a happy character who could see no difficulty about forgiveness. He believed that the only thing needed to settle all conflicts was a little common sense. If only it were as easy as that!

To forgive means that one should be prepared to sacrifice one's rights, to tear a piece out of oneself. It will mean creating a new relationship. What is past cannot literally be undone. But the future is open. We can forgive and form a new relationship.

To forgive, like the French *pardonner*, the Italian *perdonare* and the German *vergeben* is a longer and strengthened form of the verb 'give'. It is as though forgiving was giving to the power of 'n', in fact until seventy times seven times (Matt. 18.21–22). To give to others is not always easy; to forgive them can be much harder, even heroic. Our Lord has been described as 'the man born to give'. He could be described even better as 'the man born to forgive'. Those who see the specific feature of his message as loving mercy, forgiveness and reconciliation have got a point.

Jesus struck his contemporary critics as scandalous in a number of things he said and did. Nowhere did they see him more scandalously generous than in his readiness to forgive. They found him dangerously permissive. If there is to be any area where love should make us 'permissive', it is in this matter of forgiving others before we come to lay our gift at the altar (Matt. 5.23–24).

Matthew's gospel provides us with the longer, familiar form of the 'Our Father', in which we praise God and then ask for ourselves: 'Forgive us our trespasses, as we forgive those who trespass against us' (Matt. 6.12). Luke's form of the Lord's Prayer is shorter but does not fail to include forgiveness, that essential point in Jesus' programme of love: 'Forgive us our sins, for we too forgive all who have done us wrong' (Luke 11.4). Nothing shows more clearly God's love towards us than God's forgiveness. Nothing shows more clearly our love towards others than our forgiving one another.

This is the one point where Jesus expects us to testify before God what we are doing. The 'Our Father' does not propose that we pray: 'Give us this day our daily bread as we give their daily bread to others,' or 'Lead us not into temptation, just as we refrain from leading others into temptation.' The only point which calls for personal testimony about our own attitudes and performance is forgiveness: 'Forgive us our trespasses, as we forgive those who trespass against us.'

Jesus' call to love and forgiveness may very well seem like a call to self-destruction. I was reminded of that more than twenty years ago when my country still dominated world tennis. A friend of mine who was feeling rather miserable about the future of faith was watching some Australian champion winning at Wimbledon. He switched off the television set and said: 'Christianity is for losers, success is for tennis players.' Was my friend right? I thought about his remark for a long time before coming to the conclusion that he had missed the point by a whisker. The truth is that Christianity is not for losers but for those who are not afraid to be losers. It is for those who are not afraid to lose themselves for Jesus' sake, because they accept his word: 'Those who lose their lives for my sake and for my message will find it' (Mark 8.35). Christian faith is for those who forgive because they are not afraid of losing. This faith is for those who believe that giving does not mean losing.

On some occasions at worship, as at the vigil service of Holy Saturday, we hold a lighted candle in our hand and share the light with one another. But we don't lose our flame by passing it on to others. To be sure, it is one thing to do something like that in the liturgy and another to do so in what we call 'real life'. In the gospels we see Jesus not only stating the principle but also living it out to the full. He is not afraid to become a loser. He refuses to run away at the possibility of losing and being swallowed up by failure. He lets himself drop like a grain of wheat falling in the ground (John 12.24). He is ready to lose his life out of love for us and the God whom he called *Abba*, because he trusts that losing is finding.

Australians sometimes refer to some unfortunate as a 'born loser'. Jesus was no born loser. Rather he was not afraid of being a loser, because he knew that to lose is to find. His disciples are not called to become born losers but to trust that losing, loving and forgiving with Jesus ultimately means finding.

But what of our persistent failures to match Jesus' programme for us? The next chapter reflects on our sick and sinful record which should make us constantly implore his mercy.

6

'In your will is our peace.'

My people have committed two sins:
they have rejected me, the fountain of living water,
and they have hewn out for themselves cisterns,
cracked cisterns which hold no water.

(Jeremiah 2.13)

The truth will set you free.
(John 8.32)

Max Frisch's play *Andorra* is built around Andri, the illegitimate son of a teacher. He grows up in a town with people who suppose that he is a Jewish child who has been rescued by the teacher. They show themselves prejudiced against Andri and are partly guilty of his death at the hands of some soldiers, as well as of the death of a foreign woman who befriended him. In the play, the different characters try to excuse themselves for abandoning Andri. Without the blessing of Christ's constant presence in our lives, we can all be like that: prejudiced, cowardly, and full of excuses for ourselves.

Nowadays we may feel tempted to plead: 'It's the world that makes and keeps me the way I am.' Admittedly the world can seem to have come adrift from its moral moorings and be moving along without a spiritual compass. Material success is everything and failure in one's profession is a disaster. The obsessive search for possessions and pleasure leaves us with a society without vision. It may not be explicitly anti-Jesus but often looks like a society for which Jesus has nothing to offer. This mind-set or, to borrow the language of a friend (Peter Steele), this 'heart-set' which puts 'self' first obviously has much to do with the sad situation of our countries. The daily newspapers chronicle the results of a society without vision that has slipped into a society without hope.

Jesus did not come to tell us either that we are innocent or at least that we can be fairly excused. But he does assure us that we are loved and can be delivered from the evil powers and false convictions which enslave us. In many ways the liturgy and daily office during Lent put before us the whole story of the Jewish exodus and, in particular, their coming out of slavery on the night of the passover. This contemplation of the exodus and the passover reaches its climax with the service of the Easter vigil. That evening we can once again express our thanks to God who brings us out of the house of slavery and leads us through the waters to a new life of freedom.

We were born to be free. We were baptized into freedom. Yet freedom is never an assured possession. We still experience so much slavery in our lives. Sin, evil, and many false standards can enslave us. We put ourselves back into bondage and return to the house of slavery.

Which of us is really and fully free? Areas of unfreedom remain in the lives of all of us. We may try to shield ourselves against admitting this. To acknowledge particular slaveries will make us want to be delivered and become fully free. It takes saints to live the exodus and the passover in a wonderfully free way. Holiness means freedom from evil and deliverance from sinful slavery. Lent calls us not merely to study the exodus story but also to take part in the passover and exodus again and again, and so complete the process of being delivered from bondage to sin and evil.

A gospel for the fifth week of Lent warns that 'everyone who commits sin is a slave to sin'. But it also promises , 'the truth will make you free' (John 8.32–36). Jesus does not promise, 'a better organized schedule will make you free', or 'the power of positive thinking will set you free'. Rather he guarantees, 'the truth will make you free'. And the truth is Jesus himself, he who is the way, the truth, and the life. Jesus is always there to bring us through the waters. Over and over again he offers us an exodus from error and slavery to truth and freedom.

Living in Rome through the late 1980s, I experienced at close quarters the bicentenary of the French revolution with its programme of 'freedom, equality, and fraternity'. But the events that unfolded in central and eastern Europe overshadowed the celebration in France. One chilly, December morning I stood in front of the Trevi fountain to be interviewed by a television channel, a hour or so before Mikhail and Raissa Gorbachev crossed the Tiber to visit Pope John Paul II. As much as any other event in the dramatic demise of Communism, that meeting symbolized the move towards political and religious liberty in countries that had suffered so long under Lenin, Stalin, and their successors. But, like peace in our world, real spiritual freedom 'comes dropping slow' (W. B. Yeats, 'The Lake Isle of Innisfree').

In the sixteenth and seventeenth centuries Europe witnessed another dramatic turn around, the Copernican Revolution. It took time before ecclesiastical authorities and others accepted that it is not the earth but the sun which is at the centre of our little corner of the universe. Jesus looks for that kind of revolution; he invites us to live the truth that it is God who stands at the centre and not ourselves. But it takes time to believe this truth wholeheartedly and practise it fully. It remains difficult to give real assent to what the radiantly beautiful Piccarda Donati says to Dante in the third canto of his *Paradiso*: it is in the divine will and not in sin that we find 'our peace'. God's rule over our lives is never at our expense but only for our real happiness. God wants us to enjoy full and lasting peace as our whole being unfolds in its deliverance from sin and evil. To refuse Jesus' invitation will be to go away not with a jaunty step but with a fallen face and a heavy heart (Mark 10.17–22).

Nevertheless, things within us resist the call of Jesus—in a way that recalls the case of Philip Blaiberg, the second person ever to have received a heart transplant. From the time of the operation in January 1968 till his death in August 1969, forces in his body fought against the new heart which was in fact vital for his continuing existence. The case symbolizes our sinful, inauthentic self that resists Christ's call to life. Just as he weeps over Jerusalem and says, 'if only you had known this day the way that leads to peace' (Luke 19.42), he could weep over us. We resist what we absolutely need and what will bring us life and peace.

Why do we resist God's will and Jesus' call to the fullness of life? I once heard a psychologist talking about 'our felt needs'. His lecture suggests an enduringly valuable question: What are our felt needs? What stops us feeling that we need Jesus if we are to experience true and lasting peace? Perhaps we some-how think that we are good enough without his help or even that our sinful state is not so bad after all. We are not hurting anybody and nobody is hurting us. Slaves can become so accustomed to their condition that they prefer to stay the way they are.

Or else we may feel so bad about ourselves that we remain convinced that nothing can ever be done for us and that not even Jesus can deliver us from our bondage to the power of evil. I still remain saddened by the tragic face of a young man at the railway station in Cologne. He caught sight of my clerical collar, pushed through the crowd, faced me and said: 'I am lost, lost, lost.' Then he turned and rushed away before I could say anything to comfort him. Did he feel so lost that even Jesus could not help him? He was gone before I could say to him: 'Please give Jesus half a chance. He can heal and change anyone. He can even raise the dead.'

Another image suggests a further possible version of our situation. Metal coins can become so rubbed down by constant use that we can no longer see clearly the imprint indicating their value. Something like that may happen in our lives. Daily worries and persistent infidelities may rub away our convictions and ideals. In the end we may no longer be able to see the issues clearly and lose much of our capacity for moral choices.

At some point in Lent we need to face our sins and the various ways we have let evil imprison us. But we need also to hear that complaint made about Jesus, 'this fellow welcomes sinners and eats with them' (Luke 15.2)—words that St Augustine said should be written on every altar. Our lives are spent in the presence of Jesus who never tires of going in search of us, simply does not want to lose any of us, and rejoices infinitely at finding us and bringing us home to himself. Jesus does not like losing us, any more than a woman likes losing ten per cent of her savings or a shepherd even one of his sheep.

To defend his scandalous love for sinners, Jesus told three parables which Luke put together in chapter 15 of his gospel. That chapter invites our meditation.

One of the commonest and most frightening human experiences is the experience of loss. We may lose our friends. We will lose opportunities. We must lose our health. We can lose our sense of direction, that clear recognition of what Jesus asks of us. We steadily suffer the loss of time, and we lose one thing on every occasion that we choose something else.

In 'Burnt Norton', T. S. Eliot wrote:

> Footfalls echo in the memory
> Down the passage which we did not take
> Towards the door we never opened
> Into the rose-garden.[1]

How much did we lose by not taking that passage, by never opening that door, by not walking out into the rose-garden? Memory can hurt and even torture us by recalling all that we have lost.

In chapter 15, Luke's gospel gathers together three stories of loss: the parables of the lost sheep and the lost coin, and then the parable of the prodigal son. The first two parables deal with people who search for something they have lost: the shepherd hunting for the one sheep which has strayed away from the other ninety-nine, and the woman ransacking her dimly lit house until she finds the one coin that has fallen out of the purse in which she keeps her ten silver pieces. Those two stories are not concerned with the fact that the woman after she has suffered her loss still has ninety per cent of her cash and the shepherd still has ninety-nine per cent of his flock. The stories seek to evoke a sense of the loss itself—the pain which the disappearance of money or livestock can cause.

Of course, the losses are slight: only ten per cent of the woman's cash and only one per cent of the shepherd's flock. Yet such small losses can prove painful and frustrating. The recovery can be even more joyful, encouraging and heartening than earning the ten silver pieces or raising the hundred sheep was in the first place.

Jesus tells his stories to evoke that common feeling. He does this in order to provide some insight into God's merciful attitude towards sinful men and women. God is glad to welcome back the godless, the irreligious and the sinner. There is joy in heaven even over one sinful person who repents.

In those two parables of the lost sheep and the lost coin we read of lost property. The next parable deals with the loss of a person, a lost son. Unlike the preceding parables this parable has something to say about what happens to the one who is lost. The other parables mention, of course, repentance: 'There will be more joy in heaven over one sinful person who repents, than over ninety-nine upright people who do not need any repentance.' The stories of the strayed sheep and the missing coin make this brief reference to repentance, but leave it unexplained. The parable of the prodigal son offers some account of what it means to repent.

It is the story of a farmer's younger son who is anxious about his freedom. He wants independence, the power to break with tradition, to get away and make his own decisions. Life at home has become burdensome to him. He secures some property from his father, converts it into hard cash and heads off for the far country and freedom. Prostitutes and high living eat up the money. The boy is caught penniless when an economic crisis hits the country. Instead of doing what a practising Jew should do—namely, look for the nearest Jewish community where he could find help and work—the prodigal son attaches himself to a gentile farmer. He is sent out into the fields to work as a swineherd. For a good Jew there could hardly be any greater humiliation. Swine are unclean. To act as a swineherd means incessant contact with these impure animals. The boy has effectively denied his religion; the sinner who began with prostitutes ends by becoming a thoroughly godless apostate.

For his work he receives far too little food; he would love to eat some of the pods fed to the pigs. But he counts for less than the animals and is not allowed to help himself to some of the pig-food. In his hunger and humiliation he comes to himself, and decides to turn back to his father and his God. He remembers what he has lost. He will return home and say to his father: 'Father, I have sinned against heaven and in your eyes.'

As the boy approaches home, his father sees him coming, forgets his dignity and runs out to greet him. Up to that point in the story the father has said nothing—not a single word. Now he begins to speak. He cuts short his son's apologies. He is not anxious to discuss matters, let alone to impose conditions under which he would be willing to receive his son back into the household. The father does not even make some formal declaration of pardon. Forgiveness is expressed by what he does. The boy receives the robe given to an honoured guest. He is handed a ring to wear—presumably as a sign of his right to act again as a son. He is no longer allowed to go barefoot like a common labourer, but he wears the shoes that the free son of a free farmer should wear. The lost son who has come home is taken into the house for a feast of joy.

The party is well under way before the elder brother returns from the fields, that elder son who has stayed loyally with his family and given his father service day in and day out. The father comes out and begs him to join the party, pleading with him in a very touching way: 'My dear child, what do you lose through my kindness? How am I doing you an injustice by celebrating the return of my lost son?' And there the parable ends—a challenge to its hearers in the time of Jesus and to its readers today.

There is much in this parable of the lost son which speaks of our condition today. It says something about that intriguing and fatal matter of decision-making. Our lives, the lives of other people, and the literature we read constantly confront us with the mysterious process by which men and women make major decisions. Why, in T. S. Eliot's terms, did we decide not take that passage, never to open that door and go out into the rose-garden? At the climax of Iris Murdoch's novel, *The Sandcastle*, why does the hero decide to remain seated at the dinner-table, instead of rushing out after the girl with whom he has fallen in love? What happens when people take this kind of decision which can remake their lives either for good or for evil?

The prodigal son 'comes to himself'. He is in a far country, caught in a situation of hunger and humiliation. But before he can find a way out of his appalling misery, he must first come to himself. He has run away from so much, including himself. If you like, he now emerges from his self-alienation. He finds himself. No one is there to tell him to make his decision or to urge him to adopt any particular course of action. All alone he decides. He must find himself before he will find his way out of his misery and back to his family.

Now, think of the role played in the story by the other brother. A fairly grim sort of young man, he may be the elder of the two boys, but that does not stop him from behaving in an adolescent fashion. He sulks outside. When his father comes to plead with him, he refers to his brother not as 'my brother' but as 'this son of yours'. It is an insolent, hateful phrase. If the younger son needs to repent, the elder brother must learn the lesson of love. A cold, unloving and self-righteous sort of person, at heart he is not a bit better than the fellow who took his money and went away. To the elder brother are spoken those lovely words: 'My boy, you have always been with me and everything I have is yours.' The father's meaning is clear: 'You have missed the whole point! Why haven't you been happy? Why can't you love, and joyfully welcome home your brother? Why have you turned to jealousy and bitterness?'

In each of us there can be something of both the younger son and the elder brother. We may have strayed away from our God—spiritually, mentally and emotionally. We may have chosen to live our lives elsewhere, in a far country and emotionally estranged from Jesus. Or we may have stayed with our God, but without really enjoying our life as believers. We may have done our duty, and done it in a cold, unloving, self-righteous way.

But we can always come to ourselves. No matter what our losses have been, we can always repent and return. We can always go in and enjoy our home. We can always rest secure in the thought that our Father is always with us, and everything he has is ours.

The other parables gathered in chapter 15 of Luke's gospel offer an essential, closing reflection on the story of the prodigal son. The lost sheep cannot find its way back to the flock; it does not return of its own accord. The shepherd must go off after it, just as the woman must light a lamp and look in every corner before she finds her missing coin. It does not signal its whereabouts, let alone miraculously spring back into her purse. At the deepest level, we prodigals cannot find our way home to God alone. Jesus comes in search of us; we return home because he has first found us.

Notes

1. T. S. Eliot, 'Burnt Norton', *Collected Poems 1909–1962*, (Faber and Faber, London, 1974), lines 11–14 p. 189.

7

'The rational is not enough.'

All our days pass . . . our years die away like a murmur.
(Psalm 90.9)

He followed Jesus on the way.
(Mark 10.52)

In the evening of life there is no greater joy
than to have loved Jesus Christ.
(Gabriel Marcel)

'The rational is not enough. It doesn't explain everything. It certainly doesn't explain why all those people
will be massacred tonight over in Bosnia.' I was in
nearby Zagreb, listening to a doctor with the deepest
and saddest eyes I have ever seen in my life. He told
me of a refuge established in Bosnia just over a year
before—on the international day of human rights. It
was to save the lives of children, the wounded, preg-
nant women, the old, and other refugees. 'For a year
now we haven't been able to get a paediatrician or an
obstetrician through to them. No medical supplies
either. There must be hundreds of people waiting
there to be massacred tonight when the refuge is
overrun.' The doctor sighed: 'The Western world suffers from necrophilia. It counts the dead but doesn't
really care for the living.'

'The rational is not enough'—this sad summary of
our human condition came from the remarkable son of
two remarkable people, a Jew from Germany and a

Croatian Catholic from Dubrovnik. The summary touched off a whole series of questions for me. Will the merely rational and reasonable help us in times of any great crisis which we experience in our personal lives or in our society? Will ordinary 'explanations' move us when we are tempted to do nothing and remain 'guilty bystanders'? What will help us to stop counting the dead and really care for the living?

Counting the daily dead may, however, seem a sane and sensible thing to do. Surely the real news in our papers comes neither on the front pages with the posturing of politicians nor on the back pages with the exploits of sporting stars? Buried half way through we find the notices of births and deaths: 'On 14 May at St Luke's Hospital to Tessa, wife of Richard Farrugia, a son.' We can then look down the page and read: 'On 15 May at home in his 78th year Giles Featherby. Funeral private; no flowers by request.' That looks like the real history of the human race: old Featherby dying and young Farrugia coming to take his place. People are born to replace people who have died (or been killed), just as we buy new tea-cups to replace those that are broken. The food and air that old Featherby no longer needs young Farrugia can have.

On occasional trips home to Australia I visit the university and high school where I studied in the 1940s and 1950s. Crowds of undergraduates pack the small campus of Melbourne University. They now dress somewhat differently: jumpers and jeans predominate. Yet, give or take a few minor changes, they all look very much as we did in the fifties. The same, but different. The faces are all new. Of those I knew, a very few are still there as lecturers and professors; the rest are all gone. Quite a number are already dead, from traffic accidents, brain tumours, lung cancer, heart attacks and other causes. That world of the golden young has moved on like straws floating by on a stream. The psalmist catches the sense of mortality so easily evoked by a visit home to our old campus: 'all our days pass ... our years die away like a murmur' (Ps. 90.9). Stopping by my high school readily prompts the same feeling. Casting my mind back to the old days, I remember Pierce breaking away from other footballers on the main oval, John with his head down in the study hall and Bill elbowing his way through in the tuck-shop. We played, learned and fought together, and they are dead and gone.

Death must come at some time and it may come at any time. If we are going to be ready to die at some time, we should be ready to die at any time. The longer we go on living and losing unexpectedly friends and relatives, the more we recognize the wisdom in the repeated warning of Jesus: 'Be vigilant and keep watch!' Life is a dangerous business. We might want to vary the gospel image of servants waiting in a great household for their master to return. We can picture ourselves as soldiers on guard duty at night. We need to keep awake; we do not know at what hour in the early morning an officer might come round to check that we have not fallen asleep.

At the end of the day, consistently recalling how transient our existence is and how life is also a preparation for death does not mean capitulating to necrophilia. A sobering thought: our mortality is an utterly certain fact and only the unreasonable try persistently to ignore it.

The doctor in Zagreb was right, however, when he insisted that 'the rational is not enough'. If we are to cope with the truly tough challenges of life, the mere thought of our mortality may not be enough. We will need to take advice from a bumper-sticker I once saw in California: 'Think Jesus.' In the New Testament no one 'thought Jesus' better for those whose faith comes under fire than the evangelist Mark.

In some ways Mark's gospel comes across as inferior to the other gospels. Unlike Matthew and Luke, it contains no account of Jesus' birth and childhood. Unlike Luke and John, it has very little on the Holy Spirit and the Blessed Virgin Mary. It does not include much of the basic teaching from Jesus which we find in Matthew and Luke. Unlike the other three gospels, Mark ends with an extremely brief Easter narrative (Mark 16.1–8) which does not even report any appearance of the risen Jesus. So unpromising at some levels, Mark's gospel is second to none in the help and light its central chapters yield for those who face situations where 'the rational is not enough'.

Up to Mark 8.13, this gospel reports many miracles worked by Jesus as he moves among large crowds of people. Now the miracles drop away—a feature which gives special prominence to the few miracles that do turn up in the narrative. This break-point also brings a change in Jesus' company. Normally he now moves around with the core group of close disciples to whom on three occasions he speaks of his coming death and resurrection (Mark 8.31; 9.31; 10.33–34). He breaks this sombre news to them in Caesarea Philippi, passing through Galilee and then 'on the way going up to Jerusalem' (10.32), three different places which function as stations of the cross when Jesus heads south to his final rendezvous with death.

The message for embattled disciples caught in 'irrational' situations begins to emerge more clearly when we notice how the healing of the blind begins and ends this central section in the gospel (Mark 8.14—10.52). The first case is that of a blind man who receives his sight in stages (8.22–26). The second is that of a blind beggar (10.46–52), whose cure leads him to do something no other person healed by Jesus does in the whole of Mark's gospel. Bartimaeus 'follows' Jesus 'on the way'. The words are loaded with meaning: Bartimaeus becomes a disciple of Jesus at the last stage in the stations of the cross, the road going up to Jerusalem.

The two miracles bracket a narrative in which the male disciples repeatedly reveal their inner blindness. The section opens with these disciples in a boat with Jesus. He applies to their spiritual obtuseness severe words that he has previously used of 'those outside': 'Do you not yet perceive or understand? Are your hearts hardened? Having eyes do you not see, and having ears do you not hear?' (Mark 8: 17–18; see 4.11–12). They have followed him, seen him miraculously feed large crowds, and yet remain dull-witted and insensitive. Their spiritual state receives its appropriate comment in the healing that comes at once. As with the blind man who receives his sight only in stages, their spiritual insight will develop step by step. Jesus will need to intervene repeatedly to bring them to the point of accepting who he is and what following him will entail. Peter, already the leader of the disciples, recognizes something ('you are the Messiah'), but he cannot see and accept Jesus' suffering destiny. Jesus rebukes him vigorously ('Out of my way, Satan') and insists: 'Anyone who wants to be a follower of mine must renounce self; he must take up his cross and follow me' (Mark 8: 27–38).

Just as in the boat the group of male disciples show a spiritual blindness, so does Peter at Caesarea Philippi. When passing through Galilee, Jesus again announces his coming death and resurrection. The group as a whole fail to understand, are afraid to take matters further with Jesus, and spend their time arguing who is the greatest among them (Mark 9.33–34). Jesus himself continues to lead them on the way to his passion, and a third time tells the core group what lies in store for him (and them) in Jerusalem. This time it is James and John who fail to grasp what is being asked of them. Once again Jesus takes nothing back. He summons the Twelve to share the fate of the Son of man, who has not come 'to be served but to serve, and to give his life as a ransom for many' (Mark 10.32–45).

The lesson of Mark 8—10 comes through loud and clear. Jesus calls us to share his suffering and glorious destiny. But if we are to appreciate who he is and why his invitation deserves our total commitment, our spiritual eyes must first be opened. Jesus will heal us, in stages or even perhaps all at once. Then we will be enabled to become utterly devoted to him and imitate Bartimaeus by following him 'on the way'. This is what it means to 'think Jesus' with no holds barred.

For hearing the call of the suffering Son of man, the male logic of Peter, James, John and the rest of the Twelve will not be sufficient. As the doctor in Zagreb rightly said, 'the rational is not enough'. We must feel our blindness and know ourselves to be cured by Jesus. Then we will be in a state to follow Jesus 'on the way' to Jerusalem, Bosnia or wherever else he may call us.

Someone told me once: 'Nobody can experience being healed by Jesus and remain the same.' Bartimaeus might have said that, as he changed in a few minutes from being a blind beggar by the roadside to become a follower of Jesus 'on the way'.

This Chapter began in Croatia. Let it move to the Middle East and Australia and then end in the United States. Towards the end of his life a Moslem holy man said this about himself:

> When I was young, I was a revolutionary and all my prayer to God was: 'Lord, give me the energy to change and renew the world.' As I approached middle age and realized that half my life was gone without my changing a single soul, I switched my prayer to: 'Lord, give me the grace to change and renew those who come in contact with me. Let me change just my family and friends, and I shall be satisfied.' Now that I am an old man and my days are numbered, I have begun to see how foolish I have been. My one prayer now is, 'Lord, give me the grace to be changed myself.' If I had prayed for this right from the start, I should not have wasted my life.

'Lord, give me the grace to be changed myself.' That prayer of the Muslim holy man in his old age could serve very well our prayer for Lent.

Being changed ourselves is no joke. As an early

Church writer, Hermas, put it, 'God does not leave us till he has broken our heart and our bones.' Of course, God does not want to leave us broken-down, half-dead people. God wants to give us true life, the only deeply satisfying life available. Yet being changed and renewed ourselves can be painful. In the gospel Jesus calls that change 'renouncing self' and 'losing our lives'. Paradoxically this loss of life is an ultimate and permanent gain. 'Those who lose their life for my sake and that of the good news will save it' (Mark 8.35). Jesus' invitation and promise are honest and clear. He means losing what may look like everything to gain what actually is everything. In breaking our bones, it is not a minor piece of plastic surgery but a real orthopaedic job that Jesus wants to do on us. Yet being radically operated on and changed like that does not bring painful unhappiness but deep joy. It brings the joy which leaps out of Paul's Letter to the Philippians. Because of Jesus the apostle has lost everything. But he counts the loss as so much garbage. The joy of gaining Christ and living in him outweighs any deprivation Paul has undergone (Phil. 3.8).

Still I must admit that the price of being changed can seem inordinately high. The cost of being associated with the crucified Jesus may look excessive, if we fail to recognize that such an association is the prelude to sharing in his resurrection. Few or none of us perhaps will match the harsh experiences Paul went through. We have not been shipwrecked, lashed, beaten with rods and almost stoned to death (2 Cor. 12.23–28). At the same time, each of us can feel, 'I have paid a high price. It has cost me much to lose and be changed.' Nevertheless, each of us has also known the joy which comes with losing for the Lord's sake, the joy involved in letting him change us. We could well join the Muslim holy man and continue to pray: 'Lord, give me the grace to be changed.'

An old friend of mine was separated from his mother as a child. He was transported to Australia and grew up in an orphanage exposed to sexual abuse. He has spent his adult years caring for street kids, the unemployable and those who find an alternative career in prostitution, the drug trade, petty crime or the production of pornographic movies. Peter has a right to speak. 'All of us,' he told me, 'are confronted with a choice: either to live out our lives in misery, or to live out our lives in mystery.' His case is extreme, and so too is that of those to whom he ministers. But, in one form or another, life will sooner or later crucify each one of us. That crucifixion will make us or break us spiritually. As my friend Peter said, we can live out our lives in misery or mystery. We can refuse or accept Jesus' call: 'Those who want to be followers of mine must renounce themselves; they must take up their cross and follow me.' To say yes to that invitation will allow the mystery of our crucifixion to be transformed with Christ into a strange but powerful resurrection.

In the USA, a highly successful football coach, Vincent Lombardi, became famous for his constant advice to his team: 'Winning isn't everything. Winning is the only thing.' We might adapt his remark and say: 'Loving Jesus isn't everything. Loving Jesus is the only thing.'

Love for Jesus, if practised in real times and real places, is going to bring us to death. An American writer, Paul Goodman, once said that the only way for a Christian to live is to risk love and hope for resurrection. A friend of mine (Peter Steele) added: 'he assumed, rightly, that love will pin us to a cross, and that crucifixion has only one outcome.' We now turn to the crucifixion and its outcome.

8

'It's always Good Friday.'

My God, my God, why have you forsaken me?
(Mark 15.34)

He saved others, he cannot save himself.
(Mark 15.31)

'*I*t's always Good Friday, sometimes a little of Holy
Saturday but never Easter Sunday.' This comment
came from the pastor of a parish on the edge of
Karlovac, a city of around sixty thousand inhabitants
that is less than an hour's drive from Zagreb by the
motorway. Since the Serbs started shooting and shelling in October 1991, nearly fifty of his parishioners
have been killed. The front-line now cuts his parish in
half. Two thousand of his parishioners fled into Karlovac itself. They live there with thirteen thousand other
refugees. In November 1993 I watched some of them
shuffling forward in lines to receive their daily handout
of bread and apples.

We drove out towards a wrecked village just short of
the front-line, ducked behind a hill and pulled up next
to a chapel. Its roof had been blown off and the stone
walls gaped with huge holes. Up the slope was a
cemetery. 'I can't use that cemetery,' the parish priest
explained. 'Just eight days ago, on All Saints' Day, it
was hit again—this time with four shells. My second
cemetery is occupied by the enemy, just like my parish
church.' He shook his head in disbelief: 'Fancy shelling

one cemetery and occupying another!' 'What happened to the chapel?' I asked. 'A tank came over the hill and started firing at the chapel,' he said. 'A couple of our soldiers crept up through the trees, hit the tank and killed the four Chetniks in it. You can see the remains of the tank up there on the top of the rise.'

I thought of those four young Serbs dying as they made a cemetery chapel their target. I thought too of what the parish priest had told me about his young parishioners who ask incessantly: 'Where is God? What is God doing?' It all sent me back to a cry from another cross: 'My God, my God, why have you forsaken me?' (Mark 15.34).

The early Christians heard and read about Jesus' suffering and death much more often than we do. The passion story or stories seem to have fallen into shape very early, and helped to give rise to our gospels— beginning from Mark. This gospel has been classically described as a passion story with a long introduction. In a sense that gospel resembles a tadpole. From our days of messing about in ponds years ago, some of us remember what tadpoles look like: big heads with long tails. In the case of Mark's gospel the big head is the passion and resurrection story, the long tail are the chapters which lead up to it.

I can think of no better exercise for the closing weeks of Lent than a profound and prayerful exposure to the passion story in Mark or one of the other gospels. It could be our way of filling out and experiencing for ourselves that 'knowing Jesus' in his suffering, death and resurrection to which Paul gave himself with such intensity—even twenty years down the track from the Damascus Road encounter. (See Chapter 2.)

It is a great pity if we leave the passion story to Palm Sunday and Good Friday. Of course, it is moving and even heart-rending to hear the two passion accounts read then. But taking our cue from Paul would lead us to immerse ourselves now in the final chapters of one or other of the gospels. Then we will come to Holy Week and Easter, having already let Jesus in his suffering, death, and resurrection once again confront us at depth. Meditation on that story is part of our response to his invitation, 'Do this in memory of me' (Luke 22.19).

A splendid remark turns up in a Yiddish story when one character says to another: 'You can't fool me, I'm too stupid.' There is a kind of stupidity we all need, the stupidity which makes us quietly and slowly mull over the story of God's foolish love for us. That foolish love reached its shocking climax in Christ's suffering, death, and resurrection.

Matthew, Mark, and Luke take their readers into the passion story through four stages: the Last Supper, the agony in the garden, the betrayal and arrest, and the scenes of Jesus on trial. Despite some variations between Mark (followed more or less by Matthew) and Luke, the three evangelists are practically at one in recalling the heart of what Jesus does at his final meal with his friends. He expresses in advance what his victimization and death will mean: 'This is my body which is given for you. This cup is the new covenant in my blood which is poured out for you.'

Two or three verses tell the story of the institution of the Lord's Supper. We read them so quickly in the gospels. We repeat them so easily at the Eucharist. But it costs Jesus so much to say those words. Once he says them, there is no going back. Various New Testament scholars have written of Jesus' shift from being the one who proclaims the (present and coming) kingdom of God to being the victim whose death and resurrection would bring the kingdom with power. For Jesus himself the reality of that change is harsh and cruel, and no mere matter of words, let alone a scholarly comment.

Years ago I saw a troupe of dancers from the West Indies perform the passion story on stage. They danced around a wooden table and expressed through their bodies what Jesus said and pledged at the Last Supper. Suddenly they broke the table up and turned it into the cross. That dramatic gesture vividly presented the link between what Jesus undertook in the upper room and what he suffered on the hill of Calvary.

From the Last Supper the first three evangelists move their readers out of the city to witness Jesus' lonely struggle in the garden. Even more than Matthew and Luke, Mark depicts Jesus as deeply afraid, disoriented, and in a state of shock (Mark 14.32–42). Prayer is bitterly painful for Jesus. In his terrifying loneliness he reproaches his sleepy friends: 'Could you not stay awake for even one hour with me?' The words are also addressed to each of us.

Led by Judas, who betrays his master with a kiss, a paramilitary force comes through the night to take Jesus into custody. When going through the four passion stories, we do well to note the times we read of Jesus being 'seized', 'bound', 'led' around, and finally 'handed over' to Pilate. Have you ever seen a woman handcuffed to a female member of the police force, or a man with his hands secured behind his back being hustled away by two officers? These are scenes which seem to violate human dignity and freedom, especially if we believe and even know that an innocent person has been arrested. Here in the passion story we look at the totally innocent Jesus, the one who has come to seek and to save those lost in sin, bound and dragged about like a dangerous criminal. What keeps his hands tied? What leaves him apparently helpless and at the 'mercy' of those who have arrested him? Early in his gospel Luke tells a story of Jesus being hustled by an angry lynching party up to the top of a hill. Abruptly they lose their grip on Jesus. He walks straight through the middle of the crowd and goes away (Luke 4.28–30). Why doesn't something like that happen now in the garden of Gethsemane? Ultimately the only answer is love, the love that leaves Jesus so vulnerable. Love has made him defenceless, and that reckless love will not turn back.

In Luke's passion narrative, after his arrest Jesus appears before the Council (22.66–71), Pilate (23.1–5) and Herod (23.6–12). The members of the Council refuse to consider the truth or even let themselves be questioned by Jesus. 'If I ask you a question,' he complains, 'you will not answer.' Pilate seeks the easy way out. Herod will not take Jesus seriously. All of those evil weaknesses remain as active as ever: the refusal to face some unexpected or unpleasant truth, opportunism, and frivolity. The result is always the same. Jesus was victimized then and is victimized now. The first letter of John calls those three forces 'the lust of the flesh' (Herod and his appetites), 'the lust of the eyes' (Pilate's greedy desire to keep smooth control of his position and power), and 'the pride of life' (the arrogant assurance of those who already 'have' the truth). These may be human, understandable weaknesses, but they are killers where Jesus is concerned.

If we read together all four episodes in Luke's gospel (the Last Supper, the prayer in the garden, the arrest, and Jesus being put on trial), we should be impressed by what Jesus says and refrains from saying. He announces Judas' treachery. But neither in the upper room nor in the garden does he beg the traitor to back down. In the hearings before the Council, Pilate, and Herod, Jesus does not engage in any plea bargaining—let us say, by admitting some imprudent infringements of the Jewish law for which he might be flogged and then released. Nor does he brilliantly challenge and slip past all charges, masterfully silencing his opponents as he did over the tribute to Caesar and the authority behind his actions (Luke 20.1–8, 20–26). But he does plead with his God: 'Father, if you will, take this cup of suffering away from me.' It is a naked, simple prayer. There is none of the beautiful language which we find elsewhere on Jesus' lips. It is a cry of fear, and then of obedience: 'Not my will, however, but your will be done' (Luke 22.42). Jesus asks for the cup to be taken away from him. But it is a cup which he has already taken into his own hands and consecrated.

Tastes differ. We all have our favourite gospel. Over Jesus' speech and silence in the passion some may once again prefer Mark's cryptic way of putting things. In that gospel Jesus speaks only to incriminate himself before Caiaphas (14.62–64), not to save his life before Pilate (Mark 15.5).

Mulling over the four stories of Jesus' passion, Christians have often taken into their prayer Jesus' loneliness. Once he is arrested, he hardly sees a friendly face. During the night he catches sight of Peter, but Peter has just denied him three times. On the way to crucifixion Jesus will pass a group of women who weep for him (Luke 23.27). But so many faces and voices are set against him: the hostile voices of the chief priests, the bloodthirsty mob which cries out for his death, the expedient voice of Pilate as he tries to manoeuvre his way around a tricky situation. In all the passion stories, apart from Pilate's wife (Matt. 27.19) and the good thief (Luke 23.40–42), no one speaks out for Jesus and pleads his cause.

One horrific episode in the passion symbolizes the way Jesus is delivered defenceless and alone to his enemies: his being flogged, crowned with thorns and then mocked by a squad of soldiers. Matthew, Mark and John report the scourging in a single line, practically with one word. They do not need to comment; their first-century readers know only too well what that punishment does to someone. They have seen what criminals and rebels look like after they have been scourged by two men systematically using spiked whips to flay the skin off their backs.

Apparently, Pilate's soldiers took Jesus into an inner courtyard of the fortress Antonia before scourging him. Presumably there was the usual low column with a chain attached to which they tied his hands. They stripped Jesus to the waist and began their cruel work. Roman citizens like Paul of Tarsus were normally spared such torture. Jesus enjoyed no such privileges. At the end of the scourging he stood there in a pool of his own blood. Or did he simply collapse over the column?

After the scourging came the soldiers' own contribution to the passion, when they crowned Jesus with thorns and mocked him. Why should that military squad have set much store on a poor upstart who had just been scourged on the governor's orders? Presumably they had heard Jesus described (or derided) as the king of the Jews. So they dressed him in the purple robe of a king, twisted a crown of thorns around his head and ridiculed him one after another (Mark 15.16–20).

In his version of the passion, Luke includes neither the scourging nor the crowning with thorns. Here as elsewhere, he softens the terrible harshness of Mark's story. Luke has reported such passages of tender love as the parables of the good Samaritan (see Chapter 5) and of the prodigal son (see Chapter 6). The good Samaritan takes care of a beaten, half-dead man and treats his wounds with compassion. The evangelist Luke cannot bring himself to mention the terrible wounding of Jesus in his scourging and the mocking of one who reached out in pity to all in need.

Sooner or later Lent and Holy Week bring us to the heart of the passion story: the crucifixion and death of Jesus 'at the place of the skull' (Mark 15.22–37). There is something senseless and inhuman about the death of anyone. The death of Jesus, the one who is life itself, can well strike us as shocking and simply absurd.

Some, perhaps many, of us have seen someone die whom we loved very much. That memory may help us to enter a little into the mystery of Jesus' crucifixion.

But huge differences remain between his death and 'normal' deaths, at least in the Western world of today. He did not die as a middle-aged man, let alone in old age. His death did not come in a hospital bed, eased by all the helps of modern medicine and surrounded by relatives and friends. He died as a young man on the gallows, surrounded for the most part by people who either hated him or had come out of morbid curiosity to see the sight.

Some years ago I was invited to contribute the article on 'Crucifixion' to the *Anchor Bible Dictionary* (published in 1992). The invitation led me to revisit ancient sources to check all the material available on that method of execution practised by the Romans, the Carthaginians and others. The research convinced me more than ever of the terrible horror of such a sadistically cruel and utterly shameful death. As crucifixion damaged no vital organs, death came slowly after awful pain. The Roman lawyer Cicero called crucifixion 'the most cruel and disgusting penalty'. The Jewish writer Josephus characterized it as 'the most wretched of deaths'. Generally the Romans limited this atrocious form of execution to foreigners, mutinous troops, dangerous robbers, and members of the lower classes, particularly slaves. Even though crucifixion was frequent in Roman times, cultured writers preferred to say little about it. Jesus' cross was seen as a sign of extreme 'shame' (Heb.12.2). St Paul did not exaggerate when he called Jesus on the cross 'a stumbling block to the Jews and folly to the Gentiles' (1 Cor. 1.23). To non-believers it seemed and still seems 'sheer folly' (1 Cor. 1.18) to proclaim the crucified Jesus to be the Son of God, universal Lord and coming Judge of the whole world. The extreme horror of his death counted against any such claims.

When we contemplate Jesus on the cross, we cannot avoid the further fact that crucifixion belongs to the human condition. Whether Jesus had joined them or not, the two criminals who flanked him on their crosses would have died on Calvary just the same. Whether I like it or not, I have or will have my particular cross in life. In freedom I must decide to take up my cross and follow in the Lord's footsteps—along that way where there is no ecstasy. Anyone's cross is hard and it is difficult to take not only unexpected and seemingly random sufferings but also (and perhaps especially?) the distress which comes from what we are ourselves and have done. We can resist all this for years in a kind of silent revolt. The crucified Jesus shows us that unless we freely say yes to these sufferings, they will have no real meaning. When we face and accept them with Jesus, they can mysteriously become the means of growth and vitality for ourselves and others. Mark reports how bystanders mocked the crucified Jesus: 'Save yourself and come down from the cross . . . He saved others, he cannot save himself. Let the Christ . . . come down now from the cross that we may see and believe' (Mark 15.30–32). He stayed on the cross with his fellow sufferers. Very soon the Roman centurion, the holy women and a great multitude of others were to 'see and believe'. Jesus was not there to save us from suffering but to give some sense even now to our sufferings. He did not encourage either a utopian dream of freedom from suffering or rebellious anger against it—let alone irrational attempts to deny that we suffer at all. As my friend Peter said (see Chapter

7), the choice was and remains between suffering in misery or accepting with Christ the mystery of the cross that comes our way. The outcome of such acceptance will always be a transforming resurrection.

Many pilgrims to Rome carry away at least one vivid memory: that of Michelangelo's *pietà* in St Peter's. The passion and death of Jesus comes home to them when they contemplate his dead body lying limply in his mother's arms. His whole story is written in his body. His eyes are closed—those eyes which smiled at children, blazed with anger on occasion, gazed in prayer towards heaven, filled with tears more than once, and looked steadily at his disciples when he asked: 'Who do you say that I am?' His mouth is silent—that mouth which announced 'Blessed are they that mourn,' told the story of the prodigal son's return and declared at the end, 'This is my body to be given for you.' His ears are deaf—those ears which had heard the cry of the blind beggar ('Jesus, Son of David, have mercy on me'), took in Peter's confession ('You are the Messiah') and responded to Levi's invitation to be the guest of honour at a great party. His hands are torn and lifeless now—those hands which touched lepers, healed blind eyes, blessed sinners, broke the bread and shared the cup. His feet hang motionless—those feet which walked the roads of Galilee, took him to Levi's party and carried him on the way of the cross going up to Jerusalem. His heart has stopped and his brain is dead—that brain which shaped his golden words and that heart which beat with great compassion for the lost crowds and the widowed mother following her only son's body to burial.

Michelangelo's *pietà* also invites us to remember

that the passion of Jesus is more than a closed story from the past. Blaise Pascal put this truth into words: 'He is in agony till the end of the world.' A never-ending reality, the passion goes on in the failures and losers of this world: in the criminally insane, the terminally ill, the handicapped, drug addicts, refugees, gypsy women shamed by their begging, abused children, and all victims who may never have even heard the name of Jesus but bear in their bodies and lives the marks of his passion. One effective way of meditating on Jesus' suffering and death is to let our mind's eye move backwards and forwards between his crucified figure and the men and women who reveal to us in different ways the ongoing story of his passion.

At times preachers have taken the beatitudes from Matthew 5 or Luke 6 and applied them to Jesus' sufferings. He dramatized in his own story what he preached about the poor, the meek and the pure of heart. Let us not forget here a beatitude which promises the gift of laughter: 'Blessed are you that weep now, for you shall laugh' (Luke 6.21). Of course, Jesus' sufferings and death were no laughing matter. During his passion only his enemies laughed and showed their sneering delight. No one celebrated or played, except for those who mocked him and cast lots for his clothing. But he died and rose so that we might be free to laugh. Jesus and those whom he redeems laugh best, because they can laugh last. Some old Easter hymns expressed this truth by quaintly ridiculing death and hell. It used to be customary in parts of central Europe for the preacher to tell jokes during his Easter Sunday sermon. He had to make the congregation laugh and show that they truly shared the joy of Christ's victorious resurrection.

My parish priest from the outskirts of Karlovac may have found no Easter Sunday in his situation. But he did bring to mind the truth, 'those who laugh last laugh best.' The autumn weather was turning cold when we stood next to the ruins of his cemetery chapel. A member of a religious congregation, he had laid aside his gleaming white habit and put on a sweater and old trousers before driving me out to the front. 'I don't always go round here in my habit,' he explained. 'It turns me into a very good target.' Then he grinned: 'But when the snow comes, I wear the habit. It makes for good camouflage.' Belief in the good news of Jesus' death and resurrection does set us free—for joy and laughter. Alleluia!

9

'I am doing a new thing.'

Sing a new song.
(Psalm 33.3)

See, I am making all things new.
(Revelation 21.5)

Some years ago I was visiting a lawyer who lived in a twenty-storey block of flats. As we emerged from the underground garage into the basement, Bob gestured towards a door on which a large notice was hanging. It read: 'this laundry-room will close at 6 p.m., because that is the way it has always been.' 'It's the janitor', my friend explained. 'He locks everything up at 6 p.m., even though most of the tenants only get home later. Many of them don't have a laundry-machine and dryer.' It was distressing to imagine the frustrated tenants and, even more, the unfortunate janitor. He had locked himself into a rigid way of doing things, 'because that is the way it had always been'. Ever since my visit, he has symbolized for me all those who take an inflexible view on anything that matters and condemn themselves to a grey life, which is not really living and not really dying.

The introduction to this book quoted a line in which God, so far from urging the poor exiles in Babylon to have patience 'because this is the way it has always been', guarantees their surprising return home: 'I am doing a new thing' (Isa. 43.19). Jeremiah conveys a similar divine assurance in the form of God's new covenant of friendship (Jer. 31.31–34). Through Ezekiel, God promises to purify the people and give them a kind of heart transplant: 'A new heart I will give you, and a new spirit I will put within you; and I will remove from your body the heart of stone and give you a heart of flesh. I will put my spirit within you' (Ezek. 36.26–27). Ezekiel's remarkable vision of the valley of dry bones depicts God raising to new life a people who were dead Ezek. 37.1–14). The psalmist urges us to 'sing a new song unto the Lord' (Ps. 33.3). Eventually the new song comes, the song the saints sing before the divine throne (Rev. 14.2–3) when God fashions 'a new heaven and a new earth' (Rev. 21.1) and makes 'all things new' (Rev. 21.5). The Bible contains many such lovely words as 'praise', 'peace', and 'life'. But none is more delightful than 'new'.

We may, nevertheless, feel the temptation to agree with Bob's janitor and take sides with the classical pessimist of all the Scriptures, Qoheleth, who assures us: 'There is nothing new under the sun' (Qoh. 1.9). At times our lives may look so grey, dull and unchangeable that we feel that 'this is the way it has always been' and that 'there is nothing new under our sun'. It isn't always easy to hope for a return from exile, a new life for my old bones, and a new heart for a fresh relationship with God. The 'reasonable' thing is to join the three holy women who remember the enormous stone shutting Jesus' body away in darkness and anxiously ask themselves: 'Who will roll away the stone for us from the door of the tomb?' (Mark 16.3). We can feel so dead and locked in, that no exit looks possible. Who will solve my great difficulty and roll away my persistent problem? Who can unlock the door of the laundry-room for me?

The Easter news, however, is that 'he has risen' (Mark 16.6). God has done the impossible and brought the dead Jesus to new, transformed life. We are free to sing our new song, since we already enjoy a new covenant with God and will see the new heaven and the new earth. God has begun to make a new people of us. St Paul calls the life we enjoy through the crucified and risen Jesus nothing less than 'a new creation' (2 Cor. 5.17). The wonderfully different and higher form of life we have received demands language like that.

Some time ago I taught a course on Jesus' resurrection in Vermont. The students wanted to mark the end of the course by celebrating a eucharistic liturgy. At the offertory they each brought to the altar some gift symbolizing Easter. At the end of the line came two tall persons, Mimi and Matthew. As they walked up with nothing in their hands, I wondered whether they were going to produce something from their pockets. Mimi stopped and then stepped out of her shoes. 'They are brand-new shoes', she told us. 'The resurrection lets us walk in a new way.' Matthew turned towards the congregation and said: 'As my Easter gift I have a new song to teach you.' Mimi and Matthew were right. The resurrection does put new shoes on our feet and a new song into our mouth. Jesus' rising from the dead empowers us to walk in a new way (Rom 6.4) and to sing his new song of joy, 'Alleluia'.

Part of us teams up easily with Bob's janitor in clinging to 'what has always been'. But part of us is open to the new. We hunger to escape from a dead past which imprisons us and find a radically new and satisfying future. We spontaneously like new things and new people; they have a special attraction. We like the look of a new dress, a new hair-style and a new automobile. Over the years nephews, nieces and other youngsters have asked me to collect coins for them. They want fresh, shining coins, not the old, worn-down ones. We can be cheered up by a new face in our office or department, and much more by a new baby born into our immediate family or wider circle of relatives. Many people, not just teenagers, like new songs. In an age of mass communications a wonderful new song can sweep around the world. The resurrection of Jesus is God's amazingly new song, which was composed in the mystery of the Easter night and has gone round the world. That song guarantees us the chance of looking like shining coins, walking in new shoes and enjoying the fresh face of a new-born child.

My first years of living and teaching in Rome coincided with the last years of Paul VI's reign as pope. He was outstanding in many ways but not a good preacher. Even his most fervent admirers would not claim that. Nevertheless, one of his Easter sermons has always stuck with me. He built it round the theme, to believe in the resurrection we must 'think new'. A contemporary of Paul VI, Karl Rahner, once described Jesus' resurrection as the brilliant appearance of a fresh volcano which shows us that the fire of God's powerful love is already burning in the depths of our world. Both Paul VI and Rahner had the next-to-last chapter of the Bible on their side. There God announces: 'Behold, I am making all things new' (Rev. 21.5). The declaration is not hedged about with qualifications as if God were to say: 'Behold, I will make some things and some people new.' Rather the promise is for everyone and everything. The work of making new has already started ('I am making'); we are justified in singing here and now our new song of Easter joy.

John's gospel takes the theme of newness in yet another direction—towards love (John 13.34). From start (John 13.1) to finish (John 17.26) love shapes the whole final discourse and prayer with which this gospel introduces its closing chapters on Jesus' suffering, death, and resurrection.

The choice of love as our way of keying into Easter will bring us to the heart of Jesus' dying and rising. In his eternal, divine life he existed (and exists) *from* and *for* the Father. In his earthly existence he lived and acted as love personified—both towards the God whom he called *Abba* and towards all human beings with whom he came in contact.

Genuine love is always the perfect exercise of freedom. At the end Jesus freely showed his complete selflessness by not running away and leaving his mission. Love kept him there in Jerusalem and made him utterly vulnerable to those who hated him and wanted him out of the way.

Love never asserts itself, or rather it asserts itself only lovingly. It never destroys what is opposed to it but aims to transform what is unlovable, loveless and even full of hatred. In his passion and from the cross, Jesus' non-assertive, transforming love reached out and reaches out to all who are unloving and even violently hostile.

In his turn he experienced for himself the power of love. Love always renews and makes young again. Beyond death the divine love made the dead Jesus eternally new and radiantly young again. He was re-given existence in a glorious, transformed way. Love renewed 'his youth like an eagle'.

So often love looks weak and even incapable of changing anything whatsoever. But the love with which Jesus faced and went through death shows itself the most powerful reconciling force the world has ever known. In dying and rising, as John's gospel puts it, he began 'gathering together the children of God who had been scattered' (John 11.52). His Easter love draws all people to itself. Hanging on the cross between heaven and earth, Jesus stretched out his arms to embrace the world. This self-communicating love, visibly symbolized on Calvary, became an effective reality in his resurrection from the dead. He now comes closer to us than we are to ourselves. As Paul wrote, the risen Christ makes us his own (Phil. 3.12).

All those who know themselves to be deeply and enduringly loved know also that being discovered by the other not only brings them into a new relationship but also puts them on a new journey of self-discovery. Through being loved they come to themselves. In being discovered they discover themselves. What is true of our human experience holds good all the more of the risen Jesus' relationship with us. In loving us and lovingly possessing us, he brings us to ourselves in a mysterious and new way. Being known in love by Jesus we come to know ourselves.

His Easter love will not only throw light on us but will also profoundly change us. Long ago the divine love made us to be; it is the only reason anything exists at all. As St Augustine wrote, 'because God is good we exist.' What was already true of creation rises to a higher level in the new creation of the resurrection. The risen Jesus is love personified. We are made again because he loves us and with the Father sends us his Spirit of love.

We learn to love through being loved by Christ and letting ourselves be loved by him. He opens our hearts and enables us to give him the only thing he wants, our love. It was and is, of course, Christ himself who personally died and personally rose from the dead. Yet in a real sense without us the risen Jesus is 'nothing'. He needs us and our love in order to be himself, the loving Saviour of the world.

When I was still teaching in Boston and had not yet shifted to Rome, a student once angrily put to me a question that has haunted me ever since: 'What the hell does Christ's resurrection have to do with life anyway?' Some kind of answer began to take shape when one of my sisters remarked to me: 'In our relationships with one other we human beings are like gigantic sponges. We have an unlimited capacity to receive and express love.' It is this capacity to love which raises and focuses the question of our future. Our family lives may go on happily for years, but then someone dies or in some other final way leaves us. Perhaps our own powers begin to decline. The questions force themselves on us: 'Is death the end of everything which we have experienced through meaningful, generous and faithful love? Do we love each other only to have our hearts broken at the end?'

What the resurrection of Christ assures us is that the world to which we go is no grey haunt of ghosts, but a richly satisfying existence in which we shall know our dear ones and be known by them. We have the promise from Christ, 'If I go and prepare a place for you, I shall come again and take you to myself, so that where I am you also may be' (John 14.3). In these terms his resurrection 'has a hell of a lot' to do with our lives and our deep desire to find meaning through giving and receiving love. It is worth taking such love as a basis for living. One day our limited practice will be perfected and fulfilled by a love which will 'last forever' (1 Cor. 13.13).

The question of that Boston student can never be answered once and for all. It evokes not a problem to be solved but a mystery to be wrestled with constantly. One Easter supplied me with some lines of approach to the mystery. An old friend was buried during Holy Week—less than two months after the doctors had diagnosed an inoperable tumour on the brain. Life with Philip in boarding school had created a bond which was never broken and which grew only stronger with the years. I know that we will see each other again in the joy and peace of our risen life. Immediately after Philip's funeral I learned that a young friend had become a heroin addict. The evil of drugs still threatens to destroy this beautiful girl with her brilliant blue eyes and soft, blond hair. But I hope and pray that through divine grace and human help Angela will be delivered from evil and enjoy, right here and now, a resurrection from the dead. Human weakness and wickedness have pinned her to a cross. But God's powerful love at work in those who care for her will raise Angela to a new life. When I think of Philip and Angela, I know that Jesus' resurrection does 'have a hell of a lot' to do with life here and hereafter.

On re-reading what I have written so far in this

Chapter, I was struck again by the blank hopelessness of the 'reason' given by Bob's janitor for locking everything up so early: 'That is the way it has always been.' The Chapter deserves to be rounded off by a cheerful story, one that catches 'the way it will always be' for us because of Christ's resurrection from the dead. A journalist who wrote about the bombing of London during the Second World War said that the picture which remained most vividly impressed on his mind came early one morning. He was out looking around after a night of heavy bombing. He came to a small house. Its windows had been blown out by bomb blast, the torn curtains were fluttering in the breeze; the tiny front garden was littered with roof tiles. At the door was a young woman with a baby in her arms. She stood there with all the devastation around her. The journalist stopped at the gate. 'A terrible night,' he said. 'Yes, but what a wonderful morning,' was her magnificent reply.

Easter is the wonderful morning after the terrible night of the cross. On Good Friday evil did its worst. It seemed the end of all things. Christ, the most loving and loveable person we ever had on earth, died a shameful, brutal death as a criminal. His end killed the hopes of his friends. With his death what was left? But death could not hold him. He returned, gloriously transformed, from beyond the grave. He showed himself alive to those who had known him and had seen him die. He talked intimately with them and called them by name: Mary, Peter, Thomas. He came to his friends, met them in the old, familiar places and talked to them about the work he wanted them to do. He taught them to trust him and believe in his presence even when they would no longer see him visibly. Like those first friends of Jesus we have the promise: 'I will be with you all days, even to the end of the world' (Matt. 28.20). After the terrible night of the crucifixion, Easter is the wonderful morning which will never end. That is the way it will always be!

John's gospel rounds off its Easter stories with the account of Thomas' conversion (John 20.24–29). Looking back at everything it contains since its majestic opening verse ('In the beginning was the Word, and the Word was with God, and the Word was God'), it concludes: 'These signs are written that you may believe that Jesus is the Messiah, the Son of God, and that through believing you may have life in his name' (John 20.31). Yet, the same gospel then adds a further chapter on Jesus and his resurrection. Let me do the same.

An Easter healing of memories

> Simon, son of John, do you love me?
> (John 21.15,16,17)
>
> Follow me.
> (John 21.19,22)

*M*any readers of the last chapters of John's gospel notice the theme of Peter's sin and forgiveness. Three times in the courtyard of the high priest he denies being a disciple of Jesus (John 18.15–27). That sombre episode ends as the cock crows, but without any repentant tears from Peter. After the resurrection he visits the open and empty tomb (John 20.2–10). He is presumably understood to be there with the other disciples when Jesus appears, breathes the Holy Spirit into them and gives them the power to forgive sins (John 20.19–23). Finally, Peter's threefold declaration of love matches his denial of a few days earlier and brings the commission to feed the Lord's lambs and sheep (John 21.15–17).

Beyond question, John's final chapter involves Peter being formally forgiven for a recent act of cowardly denial. But the text says much more than that. It shows us the risen Jesus bringing up a buried past and healing old memories for Peter *and for the reader*. As so often in John's gospel, the text invites us to identify with the men or women who meet and experience Jesus. In this case our identification with the disciples in John 21 entails remembering situations into which we have been drawn right from the first chapter of that gospel. This is an exercise that can recall and heal our own buried past. Let us see how the final chapter of John works to that effect.

After chapter 20 the situation we discover in the final chapter is astonishing. Peter and the other disciples have received the Holy Spirit and been sent on their mission by the risen Jesus (John 20.21–22). Then we suddenly find seven of them out fishing almost as if Jesus had never existed and had never turned their lives around. Peter's announcement 'I am going fishing' (John 21.3) seems like ignoring or even denying the association with Jesus that has so shaped his recent past. At the very least it suggests deep uncertainty about the future and the way Peter and his fellow disciples should begin their ministry to the world. Nevertheless, the text evokes what we already know, not from John but from the other gospels: Peter and 'the sons of Zebedee' (John 21.2) were fishermen when Jesus first called them (Mark 1.16–20). Something of their past is showing through.

John's final chapter opens by announcing that it will describe how the risen Jesus manifests himself again to the disciples (John 21.1), his third self-manifestation after the resurrection (John 21.14). Three times in these two verses we find the verb 'manifest', the same word used to close the story of the changing of water into wine: 'This, the first of his signs, Jesus did at Cana in Galilee, and manifested his glory; and his disciples believed in him' (John 2.11). The narrative encourages the reader to remember that episode by noting that one of the seven fishermen, Nathanael, comes from 'Cana in Galilee' (John 21.2). Once again the past is being recalled. Just as Galilee saw Jesus working his first sign to manifest his glory, so now in the same Galilee the risen Jesus manifests himself as 'the Lord' (John 21.7,12).

He does so 'just as day is breaking' (John 21.4). He is there on the beach when the dawn comes and the darkness slips away. The scene evokes the cure of the blind man (John 9.1–39) and Jesus' claim: 'I am the light of the world' (John 9.5). The spring dawn at the end of the gospel takes the reader back even to the very beginning and the light which shines in the darkness to enlighten and give life to every man and woman (John 1.4–9).

In the closing chapter of John the seven disciples have fished all night without catching anything. Now the 'stranger' on the lakeside tells them to cast their net on the right side of the boat. They do so and make an enormous catch (John 21.6,8,11)—an echo of the 'life in abundance' (John 10.10) which, right from its prologue, the gospel has promised that the light of the world will bring (John 1.4).

The extraordinary catch of fish, the only miraculous or semi-miraculous event of its kind in the Easter stories of all four gospels, recalls the multiplication of the loaves and *fishes* (John 6.1–15). In the discourse that follows that miracle Jesus, speaks of people being 'hauled' or drawn to him (John 6.44), a verb that turns up later in the promise: 'When I am lifted up from the earth, I will draw [literally, 'haul'] all people to myself' (John 12.32). Now in the closing chapter of the fourth gospel the same verb recurs when Peter 'hauls' ashore the unbroken net containing 153 fish. Symbolically Peter the fisherman is now engaged in the work of 'hauling' others to the Lord (see Mark 1.17).

When the disciples reach land, they see that Jesus has already prepared for them some fish and bread (John 21.9). Nevertheless, in a way that evokes what he has done when multiplying the loaves and fishes (John 6.8–11), Jesus asks the disciples to bring him some of the fish which they have just caught (John 21.10). Then he 'takes' and 'gives' them bread and fish (John 21.13), just as he has done earlier (John 6.13). The reader is being challenged to recall an earlier story. Once again the text works to summon up a past grace by which we can be touched again.

Many readers link the 'charcoal fire' (John 21.9) around which the disciples take their breakfast with the charcoal fire in the high priest's courtyard, the scene of Peter's denial (John 18.18,25). The second morning scene encourages a new evaluation of Peter and ourselves. A broken past can resurface and be redeemed.

However, what may pass unnoticed, is the way the lakeside breakfast works to heal the memories of earlier meals in John's narrative. Those earlier meals have been occasions of deadly threats (John 12.1–11), disputes (John 12.4–8), betrayal (John 13.21–30), or at least misunderstanding (John 2.3–4). The miraculous feeding of the five thousand (John 6.1–15) leads into the discourse about the bread of life, which ends with many disciples leaving Jesus and the first warning about Judas' treacherous betrayal (John 6.25–71). The last chapter of John explicitly recalls for us the Last Supper (John 21.20). In a healing way the Easter breakfast at dawn re-evokes all those earlier meals and the crises associated with them.

Most readers have a sense of what the gospel is saying through Peter's threefold profession of love (John 21.15–17). Peter must acknowledge and come to terms with his sinful failure. Renouncing his threefold denial (John 18.15–17), he is forgiven and rehabilitated. Undoubtedly the professions match the denials. But the story conveys a richer sense of healing than just that.

At their very first meeting Jesus speaks to Peter as 'Simon, son of John' (John 1.42), an address repeated three times at their last, post-resurrection encounter (John 21.15–17). The good shepherd calls his sheep by their names (John 10.3). Peter is now commissioned to feed the Lord's lambs and sheep. This pastoral charge takes us back to the imagery of the good shepherd and his sheep (John 10.1–8). The great catch of fish with which chapter 21 opens might have shaped the missionary charge as 'cast my net, catch my fish'. Yet shepherding the flock entails danger and death (John 10.11–15,17–18). Peter's commission will call him to martyrdom (John 21.18–19) in the service of the flock. No longer is it a matter of his deciding whether or where to go or stay (John 6.67–68). He will be carried where he does not wish to go (John 21.18–19). Like Philip at the beginning of the gospel (John 1.43), at the end Peter hears the simple but radical call to faithful discipleship: 'follow me' (John 21.19,22). Right from the start, Jesus has been putting questions to various individuals and groups (John 1.38; 2.10; 6.67). The end of the gospel features the only question Jesus ever repeats, and he puts it three times to Peter: 'Do you love me?' In the closing chapter an old habit is intensified. Peter faces Jesus the Questioner, to whom he professes his love and from whom he receives forgiveness and his commission.

John's narrative shows us Peter recovering his past before he begins the pastoral ministry which will eventually lead to his martyrdom. As we have seen, the last chapter of John recalls much of Jesus' story and ministry, right back to the very prologue. Peter is taken through all that, down to his shameful failure during the passion. The past is not denied, but recalled, forgiven and redeemed. This healing becomes the basis for Peter's new future.

John 21 begins with Peter gone out fishing. He is, as it were, taking time off while he seeks for a pattern of meaning in his life and particularly in his recent experiences. It is almost as if, for the moment at least, the grand design has eluded him. But the Lord appears at dawn to heal Peter's past and enroll him in an heroic design which will lead to his martyrdom (John 21. 18–19).

Something like this process can come true as well for readers of the fourth gospel. To the extent that they have allowed themselves to become involved with Jesus in the whole of John's story, the final chapter will have its effect on them. It will bring up memories of Jesus and past encounters with him, so as to heal and redeem that past. For the readers, no less than for Peter, the 'follow me' of the last chapter can evoke and heal their memories as the basis for a new future.

This way of looking at John 21 accounts for the deeply haunting quality which many readers find in it. Somehow we have heard and experienced it all before. That closing chapter works to bring back to the surface painful and sinful memories. But they can become the start of a fresh future—through the loving and forgiving presence of the risen Lord.

Epilogue

I am the way, the truth and the life.
(John 14.6)

*P*ublishers often push authors into summarizing their latest book in one sentence. If they do that to me again this time, here is the sentence: 'We are the question and Jesus is the answer.' During Lent and at other times of the year the language of our public worship frequently introduces talk of redemption and salvation in specifying 'the answer' that Jesus offers us. We praise and thank him by saying, 'You are the Saviour of the world'; 'by your holy cross you have redeemed the world.' But how would each of us want to unpack that language and articulate the gift of salvation?

On university campuses in the United States I sometimes heard doctoral or ex-doctoral candidates described as having their 'ABD'. 'All but the dissertation', I was told when I enquired what the 'degree' meant. The most regrettable of my own ABD cases has been a highly intelligent theologian. He has read everything in sight and writes very easily. But being a perfectionist rather than a realist, he can never bring himself to complete and submit his thesis. However, he has permanently enriched my appreciation of what Christ's gift of salvation entails by interpreting it as our being liberated from three evils and graced by three blessings. Salvation is being released from death, absurdity, and hatred and redeemed for life, meaning, and love.

First, we all want to escape death in all its forms, not only the dark enigma of our biological death at the end but also all the other deadly things which steadily take life from us along the way. We lose friends, opportunities, energy, health and everything else that we either let slip or must part with, whether we like it or not. Both here and hereafter Jesus holds out to us life in abundance. He is 'the living bread' (John 6.51), 'life' itself (John 14.6). Steady and faithful union with him brings vitality to human existence which we see strikingly exemplified in saintly men and women.

Second, we find it very hard to tolerate senseless situations and even to keep going when things seem meaningless. We long to escape from absurdity and to find the light which gives meaning to our struggles and turns our wanderings into pilgrimages. Jesus is 'the light of the world' (John 8.12), the truth in person, who sets us free from meaningless darkness. Meeting him and undergoing a conversion, dramatic or otherwise, to his message gives life a new sense of direction and purpose. It is no accident that some converts publish their stories under such titles as *Now I See* (John 9.25). The prologue of John's gospel calls Christ 'the Word', a Greek term which might also be rendered as 'the Meaning': 'In the beginning was the Meaning, and the Meaning was with God, and the Meaning was God ... And the Meaning became flesh and dwelt amongst us.' Whatever we do with our translation, Jesus remains 'the true light that gives light to everyone' (John 1.9).

Third, none of us likes being treated with coldness, indifference and hatred. We yearn to be loved and to love. Daily experience witnesses to the power of love.

Those who love others make possible a change in the objects of their love, at times even a stunning transformation that they never fully bargained for. To be persistently loved can yield the energy and inspiration for a lifetime of dedicated commitment. In the New Testament no one surpasses John in valuing the dying and rising of Jesus as the mystery which brings believers into God's own inner life of love (John 17.26). In a last prayer before his arrest, Jesus prays that all may share in that love which is at the heart of all things.

If my publishers ask me what I hope to achieve through this book, my reply will take this form: 'I pray and hope that its readers might experience even more vividly the fullness of life, meaning, and love which Jesus holds out to each of us.'

Index